WITH AN OPEN MIND
# TOLERANCE
AND DIVERSITY

# WITH AN OPEN MIND
# TOLERANCE
## AND DIVERSITY

Alfred Herrhausen Society
for International Dialogue

IM F.A.Z.-INSTITUT

Bibliographic information published by Die Deutsche Bibliothek
Die Deutsche Bibliothek lists this publication in the Deutsche Nationalbibliographie;
detailed bibliographic data is available at http://dnb.ddb.de

Alfred Herrhausen Society for International Dialogue

# With an Open Mind – Tolerance and Diversity

F.A.Z.-Institut für Management-,
Markt- und Medieninformationen GmbH
Frankfurt am Main: 2002

ISBN 3-934191-77-0

**Frankfurter Allgemeine Buch**
IM F.A.Z.-INSTITUT

| | |
|---|---|
| Copyright | F.A.Z.-Institut für Management-, Markt- und Medieninformationen GmbH Mainzer Landstraße 195 60326 Frankfurt am Main |
| Editors | Susan Stern, Elisabeth Seligmann |
| Translation | Bill McCann, Igor Reichlin |
| Design | Schaper Kommunikation, Bad Nauheim |
| Photography | Anne Hoffmann, Reichelsheim |
| Print | Druckhaus Beltz, Hemsbach |
| Coordination | Christiane Girg, Maike Tippmann |

All rights reserved.

No part of this publication may be reproduced or used in any
form or by any means without the permission of the publisher.

Printed in Germany

**Alfred Herrhausen** Society
for International Dialogue
A DEUTSCHE BANK FORUM

60262 Frankfurt am Main

alfred.herrhausen-gesellschaft@db.com
www.alfred-herrhausen-society.org

# TABLE OF CONTENTS

INTRODUCTION

Josef Ackermann
Tolerance and Diversity in an Increasingly
Complex Global World .................................................. 11

TERRORISM AND TOLERANCE

Benjamin R. Barber
Jihad versus McWorld .................................................. 19

Tariq Ali
The Clash of Fundamentalisms .................................. 29

Tariq Ali, Benjamin R. Barber und Daniel Cohn-Bendit
in Conversation with Quentin Peel
Diverging Opinions ...................................................... 37

Fyodor Burlatsky
Bear and Dragon Change Course ............................... 45

Cem Özdemir
More PC, Please! .......................................................... 47

FORMING SOCIETY –
THE DYNAMICS OF IDENTITY AND PLURALISM

Soheib Bencheikh
The Separation of Religion and Identity .................... 52

Dan Diner
Colour-Blindness as a Basis for Tolerance ................. 54

Assia Djebar
The Silent Revolution of Women ............................... 57

Imre Kertész
The Problem of Nationality in Eastern European States ... 60

Harriet Mandel
The American Model .................................................. 63

TABLE OF CONTENTS

## THE CHALLENGE OF DIVERSITY IN BUSINESS

Kenichi Ohmae
Business and Culture in Cyberspace ........................... 69

Rama Bijapurkar
Competitive Advantage Through Diversity.................... 76

Peter Goldmark
Minorities and Majorities ........................................ 79

Tessen von Heydebreck
From the One Culture Bank to the One Bank Culture ..... 82

Vural Öger
Diversity in the Work World..................................... 86

Museji A. Takolia
A Matter of Leadership .......................................... 88

Paul S. Miller
Diversity and Tolerance in the Work Environment ......... 93

## FULL BOATS NOW – EMPTY CUPBOARDS LATER?

Roger van Boxtel
A Hypocritical Discussion ....................................... 104

Daniel Libeskind
The Beauty of Integration ....................................... 107

Wolfgang Schäuble
The Need for Better Integration ............................... 110

Peter Scholl-Latour
Mass Migration in an Age of Bad Conscience................ 112

Gianni Vattimo
Bel Paese Between Natural Disaster and Control ........... 114

## THE INTERVENTION CONUNDRUM

Ian Buruma
The War of Values ................................................. 118

Jeffrey Abramson
To Intervene or Not to Intervene ... ........................... 124

Peter Eigen
Zero Tolerance ..................................................... 127

Richard Goldstone
International Law à la Carte ..................................... 130

Barry Steinhardt
America: Flouting Cherished Principles ...................... 133

Ilija Trojanow
Without Violence .................................................. 136

## THE PATH TO THE FUTURE: BUILDING AN OPEN MIND

Hans Küng
Building an Open Mind ........................................... 141

Shala Azad
Change in Afghanistan: a Long Process ...................... 149

Nigel Barley
The Pull of the Mall ............................................... 151

Wilhelm Heitmeyer
The Risks of Tolerance ........................................... 154

Dr. Motte
The Rule of Respect ............................................... 156

Gilles Kepel
Hope for the European Model ................................... 157

TABLE OF CONTENTS

PERSPECTIVES

Armin Nassehi
The Paradox of Tolerance .......................................... 161

The Speakers ...................................................... 166
The Alfred Herrhausen Society
for International Dialogue ........................................ 176

*The Alfred Herrhausen Society was founded in 1992 to pay tribute to the memory of Alfred Herrhausen, spokesman of the board of Deutsche Bank, who fell victim to intolerance in 1989 when he was assassinated by terrorists. Alfred Herrhausen was a remarkable man with a strong sense of social responsibility; the responsibility owed by a large and powerful organisation to the society of which it is a part. The Alfred Herrhausen Society exists to carry out his mission: to make the bank an active contributor to the good of society, a model corporate citizen. It is, so to speak, the visible social conscience of the bank, our social-political think-tank, which gives us a platform for dialogue and provides us with intellectual stimulus. I am convinced that an organisation which recognizes and accepts its social responsibility contributes greatly to its own shareholder value. That is why Deutsche Bank is proud of the Alfred Herrhausen Society and the work it has been doing.*

Josef Ackermann

# Josef Ackermann

Spokesman of the Board
of Managing Directors,
Deutsche Bank, Frankfurt

# Tolerance and Diversity in an Increasingly Complex Global World

Each year, Deutsche Bank is proud to support the Theme of the Year of its think-tank, the Alfred Herrhausen Society for International Dialogue. The themes vary considerably, and reflect a current preoccupation of society at large. In 2002, the theme which has provided us with a leitmotiv has been tolerance and diversity.

Tolerance and diversity are societal perennials. However, there can be little doubt that in recent times they have taken on greater urgency, and demand our renewed and sustained attention. As our world becomes ever more a global village, a global market place, issues of co-existence, of living side-by-side with neighbours who are different from ourselves, are forcing themselves to the fore. They cannot be ignored or wished away. And while for many of us, unavoidable everyday encounters with unfamiliar cultures are a great enrichment, they are perceived as a threat by many others. It is difficult to be tolerant of a person, of people, you fear. The fear has to be dispelled before tolerance can begin, before diversity can be whole-heartedly embraced.

The project of our Theme of the Year was jolted into high gear by the terrorist attacks of September 11th, which focussed everyone's attention on the urgency of confronting head-on and hands-on the deadly consequences of intolerance. The tragic events made it painfully clear how unprepared we were for the kind of violence that rabid intolerance could unleash. At the same time, as a result of the terrorist attacks, many normally tolerant citizens in normally tolerant parts of the world became even more frightened of "others", of almost anyone who looked or acted "differently", and as diversity became suspect, intolerance spread like a relentless oil spill. In the initial panic and hysteria, innocent people who simply looked vaguely suspicious were harassed, and worse. As we took stock in the months that followed, we realized more forcefully than ever that to co-exist harmoniously with our global neighbours, we cannot turn away from otherness, we are required to make the effort to understand it, to respect people unlike ourselves.

To assess where we at Deutsche Bank stand on these issues, we have been looking more closely at ourselves and at the world in which we live. And it's a pretty big chunk of the world, since we have become a truly global institution. That means, of course, that we are not simply "working with" Africans, Asians, Americans, Australasians and Europeans. No, all of these different cultures make our business what it is.

Our exposure to diverse cultures is becoming a defining factor in setting the bank's strategy. The greater diversity of our customers is encouraging us to create multicultural employee teams. These teams are far better able to meet the diverse needs of our clients and reflect far more adequately the complex and changing make-up of the societies in which we work.

Diversity has become a critical source of competitive advantage, while a diverse, tolerant work-and-life environment has become a crucial factor in the global race for best talents. Only talented people can deliver new, rich ideas, conduct an open-minded dialogue and make contributions based on their diverse cultural backgrounds. We know that outstanding talent comes in all different shapes, sizes, colours, orientations and convictions, and we know that such diverse talents are exactly what we are looking for.

It is obvious to us that diversity breeds innovation. Moreover, our success is increasingly defined by and dependent upon our ability to leverage our diverse talents and use them creatively. Pluralism requires mixed teams, and all that a mixed team implies: working together in any geographical location, on any projects and at any level of the hierarchy. We want to turn the whole of Deutsche Bank into such a high-powered mixed team. A team made up of the best international talents we can find.

We aim not simply to become an employer of choice, but an employer of *first* choice. This means that diversity has to become a mind-set. We have to hire from the broadest possible pool of talent, keep looking for more and better ways to promote flexibility in working practices and in work-life balance programmes, implement a zero tolerance policy towards discriminatory behaviour. All of this must be driven not by political correctness but by conviction. This conviction has to come from the top and filter all the way down. That is to say, we hold senior management responsible for implementing a diversity philosophy, rather than simply fulfilling diversity quotas. The way I see it, shareholder value can only benefit from this philosophy, which is part of what I would like to call "culture value".

Although culture value is a so-called soft factor, and is undeniably hard to quantify, it is absolutely vital to the ultimate success of the goals we have set for our company. What's more, it makes bottom-line sense. We're working hard to make this policy a reality. Indeed, we have come a long way in our thinking and acting since the Alfred Herrhausen Society was established ten years ago, but we still have a long way to go.

It has cost the Alfred Herrhausen Society an extra effort to cope with the flow of events in the aftermath of September 11th. It has had to deal with profound shifts in public opinion and political action. A war has been declared on terrorism because the attacks on New York and Washington could not be tolerated. The situation in the Middle East has deteriorated steadily. In this volatile, frightening environment, the tolerance and diversity discussion has taken on new dimensions. The Alfred Herrhausen Society has risen to this unexpected challenge by addressing the complex and controversial issues throughout the year. Its forward-looking book, *The End of Tolerance?*, has been received with acclaim; its tenth annual colloquium in Berlin brought together some outstanding minds from around the world to examine different aspects of the debate.

The book you have in front of you contains some of the fruits of the Berlin colloquium. It was not possible to include all of the lively and often heated discussions, but we have attempted to include the highlights. Our thanks go to the participants and to the audience, who together made the event such a success.

INTRODUCTION

Daniel Cohn-Bendit, Cem Özdemir,
Benjamin R. Barber, Quentin Peel (moderator),
Tariq Ali, Fyodor Burlatsky

# Terrorism and Tolerance

*It is no major feat for people of the same colour, background and persuasion to live together in relative peace. It is a far greater feat for significantly different populations to do so. What happens when seemingly incompatible ideologies and value systems confront each other head-on? Where does tolerance come in and what can it do in conflict situations? Has globalisation, the erstwhile harbinger of global village peace, become a driving force of international terrorism? Is there any hope for a harmonious world community?*

# Benjamin
# R.Barber

Kekst Professor of Civil Society, University of Maryland,
and Director, Democracy Collaborative, New York

# Jihad versus McWorld

The questions that I plan to address are about tolerance and diversity and their role in a world after September 11th. I want to consider whether the prospects for tolerance and diversity in a world whose agenda is dominated by terrorism and globalism can really be furthered under such conditions. Particularly if we continue to spend ourselves and our energies trying to defend market globalization and what I call the forces of "McWorld" – a material, consumer, privatised, global market society – against the forces of radical fundamentalism which reject globalization, modernity and democracy. In that conflict, will we be helping or hurting the struggle for democracy and the struggle for diversity? Few people among the civilised nations around the world would dispute the importance of diversity and tolerance, of democracy and equality. But can we achieve their substance in a world in which the war on terrorism dominates our everyday agenda?

Despite what journalists have said, September 11th did not change everything. But it did reinforce powerful changes that were already underway on that tragic date. The most important of these changes was the move away from a 19th century planet of independent sovereign nation-states, engaging one another through war, diplomacy, and economics as separate and autonomous entities, towards a world of increasing interdependence. A world in which ecology, technology, new communications, economics, and increasingly, global crime and violence, fused countries together into a single interdependent entity in which no nation, however powerful, was capable of defending its own destiny by itself.

No nation had had a longer and more glorious experience with independence than the United States. This nation was born around a declaration of independence; it is separated by two oceans from the rest of the world; it is proud of its insularity and its ability to go it alone. And no nation has ever discovered more brutally or forcefully the limits of its own independence and autonomy than America did on September 11th, a date on which we were not only visited by terrorists but by a brutal new breed of tutors and pedagogues who wanted to teach us, and did teach us, the limits of sovereign power. In a post-bilateral world, one in which sovereign peoples controlled their own destinies, this nation, this hyper-power, was forced to yield to a world in which sovereignty itself seemed under assault. And in which a new global order – or better, global disorder – was increasingly becoming the environment in which we all lived – rich and poor, north and south, white and non-white around the world.

It is this new interdependent sovereignty-weakened world that the terrorists reminded us was our world. A world of what I have called asymmetrical globalization. That is to say, a world in which institutions were being globalized, but unevenly. Economic and technological institutions have been being globalized for over thirty to forty years now. We know from epidemiology that the HIV virus does not stop for frontier and border checks. We know that West Nile Virus does not carry a passport. We know that global warming moves at will, and that sovereign nations cannot individually treat its appalling effects on the climate and eventually on the economy of the globe. We know that interdependence is, for better or worse, our fate. Business, banks, corporations certainly know this. They have operated in an international globalized climate at least since the end of World War II. And even before World War I, the percentage of GNP devoted to trade was already 12 or 13%. But it's not clear that those entities responsible for our future, our governments, fully understand what business on the one hand, and criminals and terrorists on the other, understand all too well: the world is interdependent. And that to control the world means not to control the individual destiny of individual nations, but to strike at the systemic network character of the world.

Interestingly, the terrorists use the international system, international finance, international transportation, international technology to do their terrible deeds. The American government, however, responded to the strike with an attack on one nation. As if we still lived in the 19th century. As if terrorism had a state capital address. As if we could lay responsibility for it to the door of a particular nation. But to strike at terrorism by striking at a single nation is to strike at cancer by doing surgery on a single tumour. And what often happens when you do surgery on a single tumour is that the tumour metastasises throughout the body.

In this case, terrorism has moved from an outpost in Afghanistan over to Pakistan, to Indonesia, to Sudan, to other destabilised regimes around the world. It is everywhere and it is nowhere. Some Americans joked after September 11th (if joking were possible) that if President Bush really wanted to strike at the states that harboured terrorists, the first states he should have struck at were New Jersey and Florida, which for two years had harboured many of the terrorists engaged in the strike on the Pentagon and the World Trade Center. I would hate to think that the terrorists better understand the character of the new interdependent world than does the government in Washington. But it is a hard lesson, after three hundred years as an independent sovereign nation-state in which sovereign people have controlled their destinies within their own borders, to understand that that is no longer possible.

In Europe, after World War II, after a century of world wars, of Holocaust, of genocide, the nations of Europe finally grasped that their destiny could not be achieved nation by nation, people by people, and for better or worse, Europe has begun to forge a common regional character. That makes life difficult for individual peoples who have to yield their sovereignty, but it creates a stronger entity, an entity in which multiculturalism, difference and tolerance are better protected than in the old European world of struggling and contested nation-states. The U.S now needs to look abroad to the global situation, but when it does so, it faces a world of asymmetrical globalization. What this suggests is that we have globalised the economy, we have globalized trade, goods, capital and investment, but without globalizing that envelope of political, civic, moral and religious institutions which, within nation-states, has always been the comfortable and temperate home of market institutions.

There is no businessman, no banker, no government official, no citizen who does not know that the strength of capitalism has always been the synergy with political and civic institutions. And within Europe, within America, within Japan, capitalism has thrived because of that close association with democratic institutions, because it has been tempered and moderated by the rule of law, by civil society, by family and local community institutions. But we have globalized market institutions and the economy without globalizing the envelope of civic and political institutions that rendered capitalism so productive and, at the same time, so safe within the nation-state. And in those nations around the world where capitalism and market institutions were put into effect before democratic and civic institutions were in place, we have reaped not productivity and democracy, but often anarchy instead. Which is why I suggest that the new global order is in fact a global disorder – one of radical economic disparities, one of cultural struggle, one in which cultures in the Third World and in the South often feel affronted and put upon by a culture in the north which is spread through the new global telecommunications media in the form of what I have called "McWorld".

The branded goods, the television, radio and Internet programming, the software – they tend not to pluralize but to homogenise the world. I think here there is a deep, philosophical misunderstanding of the roots of diversity and tolerance. I think in the last thirty years we have persuaded ourselves that diversity and tolerance can be produced by privatised market institutions – when historically they have always been the product of public, democratic, legal institutions. Just as the private corporation is a product of public law, so too are diversity and freedom products of public law. They cannot exist independently of free democratic institutions. Privatisation celebrates individuality but actually undermines pluralism. That's the paradox of the market. Thirty years ago in America, we thought the state could do everything and the market could do very little. That was a myth, a dangerous myth. But today we have reversed the myth, and often in the west, we believe the market can do everything and the state can do nothing – and that is an equally dangerous myth. The strength of the west has been the balance between public and private, between government and markets. In the partnership between the three legs of a healthy democratic society – government, economy, and civil society – can be found the real virtue of democracy.

By civil society, I am referring to civic institutions, family, religious institutions, philanthropy, recreation, the arts. We live our lives partly as citizens and partly as private producers and consumers, but most of the things we really care about happen in that third realm of civil society. Civil society is where we pray, where we learn, where we have our recreation, where we are married and have children, where we go to church, mosque or synagogue. Civil society is the place where most ordinary men and women live out their lives. Where is the global equivalent of our local neighbourhoods and our civil society? We live in a world of admirable NGOs such as 'Médecins Sans Frontières'. One might say we also live in a world of 'terroristes sans frontières'. However, I have yet to encounter 'citoyens sans frontières'. That is surely the missing category – because global democracy will start not with global government or a global court, although these are important institutions. Global democracy has to start with global citizenship, with global civil society. It has to be built from the bottom up, not from the top down. That's much harder. If you think world federalism is hard, if you think forging from the United Nations an instrument of global governance is hard – how much harder it will be to forge something like 'citoyens sans frontières', to forge global citizenship, a form of identity in which people wear their civil hat not just in the neighbourhood, in the province, in the state, in the canton, in the nation – but also in the world as a whole.

How do we forge a form of citizenship in which respect, tolerance, pluralism and diversity all thrive in a world in which people do not see themselves as global citizens? The toughest task for Europe has not been to create European technical institutions, a European administration, a European parliament, a European economy, or even a European currency, but to create a European citizenship. Jean Monet dreamed of the European but what we have today is the Euro – and for all its importance, it's a poor surrogate. Most people who live in Europe still lack a sense of European citizenship. That's the hardest task, but I would argue that it is the indispensable task of those who wish to create meaningful global pluralism and multiculturalism because – and this is also what the terrorists taught us – we cannot afford not to. While men and women of good will struggle to create a more multicultural and tolerant world, waiting in the wings there is also a reactionary politics of nationalism and fear, rage and resentment. In Europe – in Italy, France, Holland, Germany - there are forces ready to take advantage of the fear and uncertainty that so many Europeans feel. And as we know, the politics of fear is much easier to propagate than the politics of hope. The politics of monoculturalism is much easier than the politics of multiculturalism. People prefer a politics of hope but find the politics of fear easier to pursue. And if we cannot find ways towards global citizenship and global civil society then there will be those ready to intervene – with a new reactionary politics which will dash our hopes and the hopes of people around the world.

In conclusion, let me suggest that if we wish to carry the agenda of diversity, tolerance and democracy forward, then we will have to create a global society different from the one that we currently face. It will have to be a global order not a global disorder. It will have to be a world in which there is less inequality. Here's a simple law of social science: pluralism and tolerance cannot thrive in a world of radical inequality. It will not happen. Not in a world in which, according to Fortune, the five hundred richest American millionaires control one trillion dollars. Not in a world where all of sub-Saharan Africa makes only 930 billion dollars in GNP, so that the five hundred richest Americans control 50% more wealth than the entire population of sub-Saharan Africa.

That is not a world in which tolerance, diversity and democracy can flourish. It is simply not a world in which people feel it is safe to practice Islam, Judaism or Christianity in their own home. A world in which individual cultures cannot be protected from the monolith of "McWorld" will be a world in which eventually even "McWorld" and its culture will die. The lesson of September 11th, the positive lesson of a tragic and malevolent experience, is that we on Earth are in one single boat and we will live together or we will sink together. It is no longer a world in which the rich can live comfortably while the poor live in misery. It is no longer a world in which our children can prosper while the children of the Third World have no hope and are allowed to fall in love with death. The single world in which we live can only make it as a democracy, as a multicultural world of tolerance. Otherwise, it will collapse and fall as a world of fear and hatred. That is the powerful lesson of September 11th and I'm optimistic because, in the end, what kind of a world we live in is up to us. It's our choice. Which means these matters are at our disposal and we are still in a position to make the world we want to live in.

# Tariq Ali

Author, London

# The Clash of Fundamentalisms

In my opinion, there were two options after the appalling attacks on the United States and the deaths of civilians on September 11th. One was to treat this for what it was, an act of terrorism and not an act of war. An act of terrorism, carried out essentially by a small organisation and responded to with a police operation to try and capture the terrorists who had ordered it and to dismantle their organisation. Instead, the United States said it was an act of war. This was the first time I can recall that a group of individuals attacking installations in a state has been accused of an act of war rather than an act of terrorism. And the United States went to war in Afghanistan, and ended up with a not very satisfactory outcome. The fact is, Osama bin Laden hasn't been captured and the leadership of the Al-Qaeda organisation is still intact. When the great thinker president announced that the aim was to take Osama bin Laden dead or alive, obviously his quarry was not going to wait around in the Tora-Bora mountains. He made his plans and he left. As did Mula Umar, his chief confederate in the Taliban. The only person who has been caught from the leadership of the organisation is Abu Zubaydah, number three in the hierarchy, who was tracked down by time-honoured police methods and FBI collaboration with Pakistani intelligence, which found out he was in the sleepy old Pakistani town Faisalabad and went in and captured him. So this entire war has not led to the capture of a single terrorist, because those who operate guerrilla-style internationally can't be captured this way. They owe loyalty to no state whatsoever and no one now knows where they are. The outcome of September 11th has been very serious because, utilizing these appalling events, the American leadership has decided to remap the world in its own image, brooking no dissent and no tolerance from its allies, let alone from its opponents, and they have proceeded apace. It has always been my view that the solution to these problems is a political and not a military one. We need political solutions, since the real problem is not the membership of Al-Qaeda, which varies between two and three thousand. The real problem lies in stopping the flow of recruits from professional, middle-class, educated students, not in Afghanistan, where they don't exist, but in Saudi Arabia and Egypt, where they do. We need to face the problems which confront that region. And they can be listed in the following order. The first, and I make no apologies for stating it because everyone knows it's a reality: the failure to settle the question of Palestine once and for all will continue to haunt the world. Not just the Arab world, but the world at large. And I think a very big mistake was made by the Bush administration when it decided to continue backing Ariel Sharon after September 11th, in fact, to increase support for him. This has caused consternation even among his closest allies. Who would have thought that Tony Blair would take issue with Bush? But he was forced to do it – and Tony Blair was not alone. But what I find encouraging is that there is opposition within Israel itself. This is clear from the Israeli press – and it is often necessary to read the Israeli press to find out what is really happening in that part of the world because much of this is not repeated in the Western press. Recently, the newspaper *Yedioth Ahronoth* published an article by its veteran journalist Shimon Schiffer, who watched Shimon Peres, the foreign minister of Israel, watching a Bush speech on TV. Schiffer wrote in the Israeli paper: "Shimon Peres' face became more and more wary and angry the longer Bush went on with his speech. 'He is making a fatal mistake,' remarked Peres. 'Making the creation of a Palestinian state dependent upon the change in the Palestinian leadership is a fatal mistake,' he repeated again and again. 'Arafat has led the Palestinians for thirty-five years, kept their heads above the water in the international arena. No, no you can't just brush him aside with one speech.' Peres did not watch the speech to the very end. He got up, turned off the TV and left the room, saying before he left: 'The abyss into which the region will plunge will be as deep as the expectations from this speech were high. There will be a bloodbath.'"

That was the Israeli foreign minister speaking in the presence of a senior Israeli journalist. And so I repeat: the main problem haunting us is the future of Palestine. We have to have a solution and that means a state of Palestine. Nobody seriously believes that the military might and power of Israel can be challenged by any Arab state today. In any event, the Israelis have nuclear and chemical weapons. They are capable of defending themselves. Even if they weren't, the United States would defend their sovereignty. So the notion that the threat is to Israel and not the other way around is grotesque. The real struggle is to see the creation of a Palestinian state, a real state, not a set of shrivelled little Bantustans divided by Israeli territory, permanently watched over by Israeli tanks and filled with Israeli settlements. That's not independence. No one, no country in the world, can accept that kind of independence. So it is in the interest of world peace and stability, in the interest of curbing terrorism, to settle the question of Palestine once and for all.

Ariel Sharon's talk of a hundred-year war against the Arabs, of the need for a million more Jewish immigrants – which is what he said to the American Senate – is extremely destructive. He won't be there in a hundred years time, he won't be there in ten because the laws of biology cannot be challenged, not even by him. But there will be other generations there and they have to be considered.

The second problem in the Arab world is, of course, the question of democracy within that world. And here I think one of the problems has been – certainly since the collapse of the Soviet

Union – that the United States fears that if democracy is permitted, the people who will win the elections will be Islamic fundamentalists. I challenge this view. Firstly, this will not be the case, and secondly, there are different (and non-fundamentalist) currents within Islam. Just as we have Christian democratic parties in Europe, it is perfectly possible to have Islamic democratic parties in Arab countries and to completely isolate the hardcore fundamentalists. I doubt that in a country such as Egypt, the Muslim Brotherhood, which has now broken with the hardcore fundamentalists, would get more than 30% or 35% of the vote. What would happen in Saudi Arabia is an open question because this country has never known democracy. In fact, this is one of the least reported-on countries in the world. Its regime is never discussed, either by academics or in the media, because the Saudis have a lot of money to spend. As a result, until September 11$^{th}$, there was almost no criticism of the Saudi regime. In fact, Saudi Arabia could be described as a tribal kleptocracy where one family runs the country, uses all the money from the country's oil reserves, does very little for its people and sends out Wahabi preachers from a very sectarian Islamic strain to convert and proselytise all over the world. The British Empire watched over the nation after the Second World War and then the United States took over in the late 1940s and 50s and they've been sponsoring the regime ever since. This is the country which is most responsible for the September 11$^{th}$ terrorists. They weren't Afghans, they were Saudis. Saudi citizens from the Hejaz.

Democracy, then, is a problem in Arab countries, but – and I want to stress this – it is not the case that the people in these countries do not want democracy. In fact, if you go to the Arab world, precisely because it is not openly permitted, you'll find more political discussion taking place in private life, in cafés and in the bazaars, than in virtually any other country. The poet Nizar Kabbani made some of the most savage criticisms of his own

country and his culture. So it's not the case that people there don't care about democracy or don't want it; they have not been allowed it. Under these circumstances, the worst way to deal with these countries is to wage war. I am glad that even the United States seems to be hesitating about declaring war on Iraq at the moment because, if they went ahead, they would destabilise that whole world. The notion that such a war would curb terrorism is a complete joke. This is why the King of Morocco, not known for his radical views, went to Colin Powell at the height of the Intifada and asked: "Why are you here? Jerusalem is not so far away: That's where you should be. We can lend you a plane to take you there now." And he said it with good reason because it's the double standard applied to that region which creates despair, anger and bitterness. The Unites States does absolutely nothing to intervene to help the Palestinians, but is ready to invade Iraq. These are political questions which have to be dealt with seriously.

I want to make one or two other basic points. The notion that in the 19th century sovereignty was supreme is, of course, only true for the empires. It's not true for large parts of the world. In fact, many social democrats in Britain and Germany in the late 19th century, Edward Bernstein, the Fabians in Britain, defended the right of civilisation to rule the world in terms of imperial needs. Today we have a situation where there is only one empire. There are no competing, jostling empires. Today we have the American Empire. A hundred and eighty-seven states in the United Nations; in one hundred of these states, there is United States military presence. It's an empire which dominates economically although its neo-liberal economic policies are creating mayhem in the world. Right at this moment, in the interior of Peru, in Cusco, twenty to thirty thousand peasants have been mobilising against the privatisation of electricity. Two people were shot dead by the Peruvian army and the government has now retreated. This is not the world of Islam. This is the ordinary world of the south-

ern hemisphere where globalisation and neo-liberal economics – market fundamentalism – is wreaking absolute havoc. And those capitalists obsessed and besotted with the Anglo-Saxon model should look at where this fundamentalism has taken the United States itself. Huge company crashes – Enron and Worldcom – corruption, corporate crime. The deregulation of society and the lack of security regulations are creating this situation, and it's affecting the whole world. This model is not going to work, it is failing before our very eyes. Europe beware. Look at what this model has done to the former Soviet Union and Eastern Europe, where it was imposed in the form of shock therapy. It has wrecked those countries and people are leaving en masse. Can this world be changed? People at the top never change things of their own accord. Social democracy and the reforms which took place in the inter-war period and after the Second World War were brought about by mammoth events. The Russian Revolution, the Second World War and the defeat of fascism changed the world because people felt that capitalism had to reform and change against the communist enemy. Today we have no incentive to reform because we live in a world without enemies. I don't seriously believe that small groups of Islamic fundamentalists are the enemy. This is just a joke. Moreover, it was the United States who helped spawn, created, financed, and funded, armed these groups in the 1980s, because they needed them to fight against secular regimes, radical nationalist regimes. Now the fundamentalist groups have turned against their benefactor, but they still don't represent an enemy. The real enemy is ignorance and the neo-liberal economic system which drives people ever further into poverty. Not just, by the way, in the southern hemisphere. There are many pockets in the North which are affected, and unless the system changes, nothing else will change. And the only way to bring about change is by revolts from below. Otherwise the people at the top never listen.

Daniel Cohn-Bendit, Benjamin R. Barber,
Quentin Peel, Tariq Ali

# Diverging Opinions

## Quentin Peel

Ben Barber has presented the vision of an ideal. An ideal in which North and South in the world actually live in far greater understanding, an ideal of global citizenship. This is huge challenge, too: How on earth are we going to get from here to there? Tariq Ali has delivered some pretty blunt warnings of the problems that lie in that way and urgently require a solution: the problems of violence and intolerance on all sides in the Middle East; the problems of lack of understanding between North and South; the problems of a world in which there is only one empire and nothing to counter-balance it.

## Daniel Cohn-Bendit

In the post-Communist world, there is only one power left capable of reacting globally, and which has a project, a neo-liberal project, namely globalization, American-style. I am not suggesting that this project should not be criticized. On the other hand, the Americans do have an idea as to how to maintain freedom, and this cannot be dismissed as lightly as Tariq does. I find Tariq's ideas for fighting terrorism really a joke. Of course fundamentalism cannot be overcome by military means, but there are moments in history when war becomes inevitable, and the attack on the United States was such a moment. Of course the Americans were partly responsible by contributing to the rise of fundamentalism in the first place. But after Afghanistan had declared war by announcing its intention to seize power in Pakistan and Saudi Arabia, intervention was the only option. And those who believe that they know how police action could work in this case, well, they are all frustrated local police chiefs who think they know something about running the world.

It is true that as long as we have no system of global checks and balances, the world cannot develop reasonably. And one power which is vital to a global checks and balances system is the European Union, because it provides a social and ecological alternative to the American globalization project. So I cannot go along with Tariq's plea for a solution from the bottom up. The constantly repeated battle cry, change the world from below! My god, just as much damage is done from below as from above! Let's not be so complacent. We need a middle way, then maybe we won't continue to make such a mess.

Again – we need a checks and balances system to counter the American political and economic project. We need to develop regional political cooperation as represented by the European Union. The world cannot be viewed as just an economic entity. We can't go on seeking nothing but economic benefit and opportunity from China to Saudi Arabia, from Chechnya to Afghanistan, forgetting about human rights and democratic development whenever the head of some Western state shows up. With this kind of morality, how will we, the Western world, ever be able to credibly advance democracy and the fight against fundamentalism and other totalitarian ideologies? We do the opposite of what we preach. And the rest of the world knows it.

## Tariq Ali

Dani and I disagree on the war and interventionism in the modern world. We have argued about it for the last five years and we will carry on arguing about it; he thinks he will convince me, I hope I can win him back over to my side. The more important question I raised was, what has happened in Afghanistan and the surrounding countries since intervention? And wherever you look, you see destabilization. You see anarchic, regional powers. What is the best way to get rid of these regimes? In my opinion, the best way is through an organic development of popular consciousness, however long it takes in these countries. Obviously there are some exceptions but, by and large, it's the best method and I'll give you one example: Iran. In Iran, the clerics took over power in 1978/79, after huge upheaval. I will not dwell on why this happened, how the United States defeated democratic forces in the 1950s. The clerics have now run Iran for nearly thirty years. Today, 60% of the Iranian population is under 25 years of age, and 70% of Iranian society is under 35 years of age. So to these young people, the Shah of Iran belongs to a fairy tale. What they know is the life they have experienced under the clerics. And they're resisting it. The intelligentsia in Iran is blossoming today. Read what Habermas wrote after he visited Iran. Organic change is taking place and it could lead to one of the biggest reformations in the religion that we have ever seen. People have learned from their own experience and that is always the best teacher, not foreign interventions and certainly not Western interventions.

## Benjamin R. Barber

Let me say as a critic of my own government, as someone well to the left of Clinton, that listening to critics abroad often pushes me to the right of George Bush. America makes a convenient whipping boy for everyone else's problems. I sometimes wish there was as much self-criticism elsewhere as there is in the United States.

To Tariq's comments on the Middle East question; the global situation is not a function of a solution in Palestine. I think it's the other way round. If we solve some of the global problems, the Palestinian issue will be easier to mediate. If we make the Palestinian question an obstacle on the way to dealing with globalisation, we're going to have a problem. But let me just correct a couple of things. Clinton didn't stop the process, and George Bush did not say, "I'm not going to continue the process." The process was stopped by the complete rejection by the Palestinians of what had happened not just at Camp David but at Tabah, afterwards. With regard to the press, the Perez comments on the Bush speech were reported on the front page of *The New York Times* and on CNN all day long. So the notion that the American press doesn't cover these things is absurd. What I'd like to know is why the Egyptian press is still reporting that 4,000 Jews did not go to work on September 11th and that Mossad was behind the attack on the World Trade Center? Why 60% of the Egyptian population continues to believe that outright, tragic, scandalous lie? Why Tariq Ali himself in his book says we do not really know who is behind September 11th, and there are no serious facts that establish the identities of those who attacked the United States? That is a different kind of fallaciousness that we also need to address if we're going to address the limitations of the United States. Yes, the Israelis have the atomic bomb. They also have tanks and F-18s. It has been to their credit that in responding to the terrorist acts against the civilian population, they have not used them. The

Israeli response has been extraordinarily self-limited. I'm against the settlements, I'm against the occupation, I think they have contributed to the awful situation. I think Sharon represents the most unfortunate kind of government for Israel, almost as unfortunate as Arafat's government is for Palestine. One would be tempted to say that the two of them deserve each other, if there weren't such terrible consequences for world history. But to say that because Israel has the bomb, because it has a military establishment, it is entirely to blame for the cycle of violence there, is to create an unfair situation.

## Daniel Cohn-Bendit

Nobody would argue that the solution for the democratisation of Iran is an intervention. Nobody would deny the responsibility of the Americans and the Russians in the destabilisation of the world. Of course military intervention in Afghanistan is not the solution to the problem, but it was necessary to move towards a solution. And the big difference between the Americans and the Europeans is that the Europeans are the only ones with a clue how to nation-build, a clue how to stabilize a region which has been completely wrecked by fundamentalism and by war. They are doing it in former Yugoslavia, they are doing it now in Afghanistan. It is difficult; look at Kosovo, at Macedonia. Small steps towards stabilisation. Of course this all takes time. Iran is a good example of how Americans, Russians, French, Germans and Europeans are making the mistake of not doing enough to help civil society take the last step. Because the last step in Iran is to get rid of a totalitarian power after a 75% vote against it. The last step towards democratisation in Iran has been halted for fifteen years. Why? Because we have no strategy – and here we agree, Tariq – no strategy which says how economics and democratisation should be much more linked than they are now.

## Benjamin R. Barber

One comment about the United States as the world's policeman. Europe, in particular, wants it both ways with America. It wants American troops in a hundred countries; it wants America to be the world policeman. But when it comes to courts and trials and land mines, it wants the United States to be Luxembourg. And it wants the United States to play by the rules of a small passive country that does nothing. I wish we had signed the land mines treaty. I wish we had signed onto the new criminal court. But there are good reasons why the world's policeman finds it difficult to do that. Europeans should not engage in hypocrisy.

## Quentin Peel

America has real problems in coming to terms with the world you describe, Ben. I think that's part of the problem. It is an American problem. September 11th didn't change the world, but by god, it changed America. It was a real shock to America. The rest of us said, hang on, I think we've been living with this for a long time. But to return to tolerance and fundamentalism. Can we be tolerant of fundamentalism? In a way, that was the question that the Dutchman Pim Fortuyn was asking, in a very peculiar and sometimes rather nasty way: Do we tolerate the intolerant or should we be equally intolerant? Do we say, all terrorism

is totally evil whatever form it takes? Or do we need to understand the causes of terrorism in order to tackle it?

## Tariq Ali

I have been deeply hostile to all forms of religious fundamentalism for a very long time. Many of us who warned against the rise of these groups in the 1980s and what they were doing to our countries were completely ignored. And you have to understand that in the guise of Islam most of these groups did not spring from below, they were not the result of some spontaneous combustion. They were created by the state, and backed by world powers, to carry out certain effective measures which they felt could only be carried out by these groups. So I've never been in favour of them. I think all state aid to them should be completely cut off and I think that Pakistan is now facing a very big problem in this regard. But I think Ben misunderstood me. The point I was making about the American and the European press is that often what is reported in the Israeli press is much, much more radical, more informative, more educated, than what appears in the United States. I did not want to make a blanket statement, I was referring to one particular issue. And of course, I agree with Ben.

There are crazy people who believe that the September 11th attacks were carried out by Mossad. There are some people – there is a French book which is on the bestseller list – that say the hits were actually carried out by the United States themselves, more or less, especially the hit on the Pentagon. There is not much anyone can do about conspiracy theories. They exist in every culture.

## Daniel Cohn-Bendit

I don't believe in Hollywood. I don't believe in the market. I don't believe in God. And I don't want anyone to tell me that the only alternative is Hollywood, the market or God. I think emancipation of the human being can make another world without our being pro-Hollywood or pro-God. That's what I'm fighting for.

# Bear and Dragon Change Course

## Fyodor Burlatsky
Chairman, Scientific Council for Political Studies, Moscow

A conflict between civilizations is very dangerous. So, while joining forces to fight terrorism, we must make sure we don't trigger a real war against the Third World, against the Islamic civilization. What should we do instead?

Let's look at how Russia and China have handled their social and economic changes in the past decade. It's axiomatic that market and democracy are very closely correlated and can help or hinder each other's development. Russian economy and society have been going their separate routes, while China's society is transforming itself at a slower rate than its economy. As a result, both countries, in different ways, are moving toward the market system, with Russia, perhaps, having more freedom but less real market, because corruption of its economy is still rampant. Meanwhile, China's democracy is less pronounced but its market economy has been a great success.

We have to bear in mind that when changes are brought about in old civilizations such as we have in Russia, China or Islamic countries, the relationship between democracy and market is not so simple. I think that we must be very careful with our aspirations to fight international terrorism through military means. Not only does this go against our moral principles, but it can also be counter-productive. We must try to help genuine evolution inside every civilization, including Islam. Only then can we hope to see these countries join modern civilization with its advanced technology, civil society, democracy and a true market economy.

# More PC, Please!

## Cem Özdemir
Bündnis 90/Die Grünen, Berlin

With regard to the conflict between Israel and the Palestinians: in my opinion, the greatest error committed by the Bush administration was that they didn't continue along the diplomatic path that President Clinton was pursuing when he had to stop. By the time Mr. Arafat got round to accepting the Clinton offer, it was too late. So, while I agree that there have been human rights violations on the Israeli side, I believe it is one-sided not to mention the violations on the Palestinian side. The Palestinians have a major problem, and his name is Arafat. The Middle East crisis is certainly one that has to be solved, because until that happens, we will be unable to solve the even more complicated problems that exploded on September 11th.

Can we talk about left or left-liberal policy after September 11th? The real question is not whether the Americans should or should not have intervened in Afghanistan. The real question, the one we politicians on the left have to ask ourselves, is: where were we all before September 11th? The Taliban regime was there before September 11th. Where were we in Rwanda? What are Africans worth? Are they worthless, and do we take notice of them only if they attack us? Is that when we register their existence? Or do human rights apply to people regardless of their race and religion? A lot of Muslims have a feeling that there is a double standard in the world. Take Germany, the country in which I have lived for 36 years and the country of which I am a citizen. Let me say a word about tolerance in Germany. After September 11th, a group of experts invited by German Marshall Fund came to Germany and met high-ranking members of German society. The topic under discussion was what happened on September 11th. The Americans said that there were many Muslims among those who lost their lives in the World Trade Center. The Germans were surprised. "Muslims? You mean the janitors and cleaners." The Americans looked shocked: "What do you mean, cleaners? We're talking about professionals, company owners, engineers." The Germans couldn't imagine that a Muslim might be an engineer. This says a lot about my society.

Recently, I was recruiting for my party, the Green Party, and forty-two German citizens of Turkish origin signed up as members. A major Hamburg-based news magazine headlined the story: "Özdemir Brought His 42 Turks". The word 'Turk' in this context was not a compliment. If this had been *Newsweek* or *Time Magazine* and the story had been an American one, the equivalent headline would have been: "The Democratic Congress Person Brought His 42 Negroes". How would that go down in the United States? We Germans often joke about American political correctness, but I just wish we had more of it here. I am often asked by new party members: "How many generations does it take for a taxpaying, honest foreign-origin citizen to be accepted as a citizen?" And the answer is that it is not enough just to be a good citizen. Something else is required. And that something else was stated plainly by the federal interior minister, who said recently in a newspaper interview: "The Turks have to be assimilated". We have to be assimilated. It is not enough that we accept the German constitution, it is not enough that we learn the official language, it is not enough that we accept the mainstream education system. That all goes without saying, that is beyond discussion. However, I want to be accepted in this society without being forced to forget the language of my parents. I will not be forced to change my religion. I will not change the colour of my skin or of my blood. And that is the catch: the colour of a person's blood is very important in Europe. It is not for me.

Dan Diner, Assia Djebar, Stephen E. Hanson (moderator),
Imre Kertész, Harriet Mandel, Soheib Bencheikh

# Forming Society – The Dynamics of Identity and Pluralism

*Identity – individual, ethnic, religious, national – is becoming increasingly more complex in our global world. The ability to accept diversity, to welcome pluralism and to show true tolerance towards those with identities very different from our own appears to require a strong sense of self, a stable individual identity, as well as a unifying national one. How can we anchor our identities in such a way as to foster peaceful co-existence?*

# The Separation of Religion and Identity

## Soheib Bencheikh
Grand Mufti, Marseilles

The notion of identity is both important in human existence, and also dangerous. Diverse identities can be enriching – diversity is always enriching. But identity linked to religion is another matter – in my opinion, the two should always be kept strictly apart. This separation does not weaken religion – on the contrary, if religion is stripped of notions of other identities, of national identity, it becomes what it should be: quite simply, a message for humanity. Religious and national borders do not correspond. An Algerian can be an atheist, a Swede a Muslim.

There is another danger in the linking of identity and religion. Religion is always understood in terms of a theology. If the theology happens to be in harmony with the times, with the historical moment and place, then religion can be positive. If, however, the theology is out of step with the times, if it belongs to another era, then all religions derived from it become archaic. And in that case, the link between identity and religion can cause whole nations to exist in a world into which they don't fit. This is often the case in the Muslim world. When Muslim countries became independent, almost all of the populations opted for a modern political system, for democratic rule of law. The countries became constitutional monarchies or other kinds of democracies – but only in theory, of course. In practice, this didn't happen because Islam was chosen as the state religion. There was no separation of church and state. This could still have worked out well – there are enough examples in Europe of countries with state religions. But a non-separation requires that the theology be completely reformed to be in tune with the times – and this has not happened in the Muslim world. Islam today does not preach a modern state. There is no democracy, no popular vote, just a pledge of allegiance. There is no nation-state distinct from civil society – there is only the prince. And such countries are condemned to remain in the 9th or the 13th centuries when the theology was first formulated. The Muslim state is in the process of teaching its own demise, because its people either go along with it unquestioningly, or they are denied citizenship.

…Not only should religion and identity be kept apart in my opinion, but so should identity and history. History is nothing but the playing out of human lives, events in the life of mankind. I live in France, I have a French-born daughter. How should I talk to her about history? When we discuss Charles Martel, who repulsed the Arabs in Poitiers in 732, should she put herself on the Arab side, or identify with Martel, the father of French identity? She needs a way out, she needs to be able to discover her identity in more than just history: in culture, customs, language, in the modern world. If most of us were able to find our identities this way, we would have a much easier time constructing a unified human identity with a common ethic.

# Colour-Blindness as a Basis for Tolerance

Dan Diner

Professor of History, The Hebrew University of Jerusalem, und Director, Simon-Dubnow-Institute, Universität Leipzig

The concept of tolerance, which we should make more sensible use of today in an increasingly globalised world, differs from the classical 17th-century concept of tolerance formulated by John Locke. But both ideas of tolerance have one thing in common in their different periods: tolerance presupposes the confessionalisation of religion. In this way religion becomes a private instead of a public matter. Christian, or rather Western society has completed this process over more than 400 years, even though it has been more by good luck than good management. Other civilisations have also been through this process. For a great and rich civilisation like Islam it is a powerful challenge to sever the traditionally understood unity of state and religion, to transform religion increasingly into confession, to privatise it, as it were. This is a precondition for the global and universal integration of the Islamic community.

On the one hand, globalisation and universalisation need institutions, on the other, the nation state is by no means transcended by this process. Anyone who believes that the European Union is something different from the old nation state is wrong. It is what one might call the nation state on a higher plane, a super nation state. But the idea of universal nationality should be treated with scepticism. Nationalities regulate our sense of belonging. Like currencies, they should not become inflated as a result of random overdistribution. After all, citizenship also implies care and protection. We will still, even in a globalised and universalised world, continue to live according to terrestrial, tellurian and territorial principles. That is a kind of anthropological certainty. To that extent the principle of the existence of the state continues to be an important element. What the internal constitution of this community should be is another question. In this process the community should increasingly liberate itself from questions of origin, whether religious or ethnic. For such an idea of tolerance the concept of internalisation is useful – a kind of privatisation and "confessionalisation" of things that are conceived as unalterable. Just as we internalise the emblems of religion, we will also come to "internalise" emblems of origin, outward appearance and so on. By means of this kind of neutralisation we would become "colour-blind" in the face of difference.

Even – and precisely – in a globalised world we must realise that stability is not everything, but that without stability everything is nothing. The intervention of the United States in Afghanistan was, in spite of all the imperfections of the undertaking, a step in the right direction. In this way a territorial community was restored. For without freedom there is no peace, without peace there is no prosperity. It is a continuously self-perpetuating error, particularly from the European perspective, but also the perception of America from the perspective of other traditional cultures like Islam, to see the United States as a nation state like all the others, even if it is one that has grown too large, whereas the United States is something completely different. Looked at closely, it is not a super-power either. The United States is, rather, another world. In the 1920s, the text of the advertisement for a shipping company ran as follows: "The world is small. America is big."

When we look at the United States and its proverbial pluralism, we are dealing with a community which has "neutralised" the origins of its citizens, who were mostly immigrants or refugees. A culture of colour-blindness to the black, the yellow and the brown has developed there: tolerance of a fundamental kind. To this extent the United States is the future of the world, and our reactions to the United States are reactions to our own future. Seen from this perspective, America is more a time than a place.

# The Silent Revolution of Women

## Assia Djebar
Author; Lecturer, Department of French, New York University

In the early 1990s, Algeria went through a period of great violence, violence which has not been entirely resolved to this day. The rise of fundamentalism in the 1980s resulted from the failure of domestic politics, from the abuse of power which was first in the hands of a single political party and then became military power which increasingly exploited the people. However, during these years, there were many who still remembered the fight for independence, men whose sons were brought up with the notion of resistance. This was a unique situation in the Third World. So it is not surprising that a fundamentalist opposition to the political corruption grew on fertile soil, and that while it eventually got out of hand and became savage, it was nourished by popular disenchantment coming from areas of poverty. It made no difference if they were Berber or Arab quarters, they were poor. At the same time, Algeria as a whole was doing well from its oil sales.

Of course, at an early stage, at the time when the electoral process was abandoned, there should have been an outcry. What in fact took place was a silent revolution of the women. One of the extremely positive results of Algerian independence was the secular education of young people, boys and girls together. In 1962, girls were accorded equality throughout the school system, from primary school to university. This was revolutionary in Algerian society. But when the fundamentalist FIS became the sole ruling party, one of the first measures it took was the banning of mixed education. However, already by the end of the 1970s, 60% of all doctors were women, most of them from the small Algerian middle class. Even the daughters of peasants became doctors and journalists. I believe that the profound change in the secular education of Algerian women is the real silent Algerian revolution. And that is why I maintain that after all terrible years of the 1990s, during which it seemed entirely likely that the secular Algerian republic would become an Islamic republic, it was the women who kept Algeria secular, and thereby guaranteed the future of the country.

...The silent revolution is profound change that has been taking place beneath the surface. It is not visible. As a result of the fundamentalist violence, of unworthy leadership, Algeria appeared to be a nation of victims. But it is what is happening beneath the surface which counts: the erosion of the patriarchal society. This process continues to cause contradictions in family life, and in fact, led to fundamentalist fanaticism. In the 1980s, the fact that women were working outside the house (often to support the family) caused a kind of madness among their male relations. These males felt that they had to guarantee the physical integrity of their women. So the situation became bizarre: the men forced the women who were supporting them to put on the chador, while they themselves claimed to be "supporting the walls", to quote an Arab expression. And this was very difficult for many of the women, women who were not always young, women with families, but women who had gone through a modernising evolution, an individual evolution, and who found themselves in the middle of familial violence. Women, especially in the poorer areas, lost their lives simply because they refused to put on the chador. To date, there have been around 150,000 victims of the civil war, many of them women. But still, there continue to be women who work, who teach, who have important jobs. At the same time, there is rarely a woman to be seen in a public space. This is why the outside image of Algeria is distorted, a caricature. Globalisation and the media fail to register what is going on beneath the surface. Women in the Arab world have been making progress – not as much as in the occidental world, but some progress nevertheless. There have been feminist movements since the 1920s. The culture is evolving.

# The Problem of Nationality in Eastern European States

## Imre Kertész
Author; Winner of the Nobel Prize for Literature 2002, Budapest

For decades, the countries of Eastern Europe have suffered serious damage to their feeling of national identity. They have to compensate for this today in order simply to affirm their own existence. As a result, it is above all non-collective values, that is individuality and individual identity, that are being subordinated to the collective in Eastern Europe. People there are used to having everything run by the state. After the fall of Communism, a large number of people who had played a very important role for the ruling elite suddenly lost their importance and their status completely. To regain this, they need a new ruling elite, a new state that hands out recognition from above, and in this way a new ruling elite, based on values which are as false as those of their predecessors, comes into existence. This produces an undercurrent of conflict between the people who want to create a state based on true democracy, and those who need a nation state and are prepared to do anything to get it.

Ever since the fall of the Austro-Hungarian monarchy there has been an unsolved problem of nationality in the Eastern European states. Their identity crisis derives – as so often – from fear. The states on the Eastern European border feel themselves to be superfluous. That creates fear. And fear is always intolerant: precisely because they did not win their freedom for themselves, and because their values, which mainly served as a strategy for national and individual survival, suddenly appear to be useless – if not shameful collaboration. It is for this very reason that a considerable section of these societies felt that the freedom which had just fallen into their laps was in reality more a kind of collapse. It would be useful for Eastern European states to have help from western societies. But Western Europe has just started down the path of right-wing populism. And this is absolutely fatal for the countries in Eastern Europe, which are going through a process of educative development.

Regrettably, it has become fashionable once again to define identity in terms of the collective. This means that the individual swiftly becomes absorbed in this collectivity. He takes refuge in a new identity; instead of coming to terms with reality, with his own deeds and misdeeds, his own history, he loses the continuity of his own life. I call someone like this a person without a destiny. The most important thing for him is not to be confronted with his own existence; as a result he will never be able to free himself from the very dangerous mode of defining identity which is currently prevalent in the world.

A European identity is derived from a number of defective or – depending on the processes one has survived – rejected identities. I am a Hungarian, born a Jew in Hungary, I have been in a German concentration camp. I write about the Holocaust in Hungarian, a language that actually rejects awareness of the Holocaust. In this way I have acquired an international audience, mainly a German audience, through my writings. I recently moved to Berlin, and because of this have become something of a

Berliner. As a Berliner I live in a city which is the capital of Germany, but also the capital of a European Union country. Thus I have also become a European. That is the result of a long process, during the course of which I have constantly had to rethink my destiny. I am not a religious Jew, not an Orthodox Jew, not a Zionist Jew. I am a European Jew who can talk and write about the experience of the Holocaust. As a Hungarian, I am not a nationalistic Hungarian. On the contrary: since I was excluded from this society even as a child, and since all sorts of things resulted from this fact – even after the end of Communism they did not try to reappraise the Holocaust in Hungary – I had to rethink my identity constantly. Only in this way can I write independently and freely. Only in this way could I discover my identity. Many of my colleagues in Eastern Europe are not so fortunate.

# The American Model

Harriet Mandel — Director, Israel and International Affairs, Jewish Community Relations Council, New York

Only a society which accepts and respects personal identity and which fosters a culture of inclusion can hope to further the cause of tolerance. I am a Jewish-American – the first-born daughter of Eastern European parents who immigrated to America before the Holocaust because, as Jews who may have been tolerated as a minority, they were marginalised and really never accepted in the society in which they lived. In America, my parents found not only tolerance, but acceptance. And because America was established as an immigration society which prides itself on being multi-ethnic, multi-racial, multi-religious and multi-cultural, the story of hyphenated identities of American-Latinos, Black-Americans, Asian-Americans, and of the scores of sub-groups which now represent the new diverse face of America, is similar to my story. Europeans used to constitute the major stock from which America drew its original character, and for that we owe a great debt to Europe. Latinos, however, now make up 45% of Americans. They and other new ethnic groups have entered all sectors of society and their contributions to American life are widely felt and much appreciated. This is certainly the case in New York, a place which overflows with pride in group identity. The men in my family can wear their yamukahs in the streets, just as the Africans wear kenti cloths, Hindus saris and so forth - without self-consciousness and certainly without fear. I speak casually about my strong Jewish identity, my religious observance - because I am an orthodox Jew - my ardent support for the democratic Jewish state of Israel and other particular Jewish concerns with the many non-Jews I meet in the workplace and elsewhere, as freely as I discuss the recent concert, or a Broadway play I just attended. And this openness is reciprocated. I recognize that the American model is not wholly applicable for other societies with different histories and experiences, and certainly the European experience is very different from ours. However, I draw on the American example, because, for all its flaws, and there are many (anti-Semitism exists and race is a particularly stubborn challenge), America, by and large, accepts and confronts its faults and works diligently to correct mistakes and foster a culture of diversity and acceptance of diverse groups. We are deeply self-critical. As Nathan Glaser and Daniel Patrick Moynihan said, we are beyond the melting pot of assimilation. In America, individual and group identity is blended with a national identity of cohesion forged by values such as freedom, democracy and opportunity. These are anchored in the American constitutional tradition and protected by equal rights, equal opportunities as well as social and legal safeguards. But rights and citizenship alone do not ensure societal tolerance. Attitudes, education, cultural norms and institutionalization of acceptance across all levels of society work toward achieving that goal. And it is hard and incessant work. Indeed, the blurring between public and private identities in American culture furthers the comfort of the individual to live his or her group identity on the outside. Multiculturalism is widely valued and broadly practiced. America is still a great evolving experiment and is, in my experience, open to change and adaptability. The challenges are great and we are continually evolving. To reinforce acceptance, we provide mechanisms

for economic and social mobility which benefit society at large. We also foster involvement in institutions such as voluntary associations and coalitions. These help bridge differences by focussing on common interests and quality of life issues. America has worked for Jews in an unprecedented way in our history, as it has worked for so many who come to our shores. The flow of mankind across continents requires change and adoption of new models and attitudes, which accept and respect, as well as tolerate, diverse individuals and groups.

Kenichi Ohmae, Vural Öger,
Museji A. Takolia, Tessen von Heydebreck,
Rama Bijapurkar, Peter Goldmark (moderator)

# The Challenge of Diversity in Business

*Studies and experience show that diversity in the workplace makes bottom-line sense and contributes to the desirability of a location. Reality, however, shows that many businesses in both the public and private sectors remain selective in their hiring and promotion policies. Discrimination is often subtle and true equal opportunity remains a goal on the horizon. How distant is it and what is being done?*

# Kenichi Ohmae

Chancellor's Professor of Public Policy, School of Public and Social Research, University of California, Los Angeles

# Business and Culture in Cyberspace

Globalisation is a physical phenomenon and it is here to stay because now the four most important resources and components of a national economy – the four "I"s: information, investment, industry and individuals – can cross national borders freely.

There are many aspects and forms of globalisation. Geopolitics is clearly the key aspect. But globalisation of industry is just as important: Internet, mobile phones, supply chains, logistics and business-to-business exchange – all these are platforms that play a vital role in the globalisation process.

A further aspect of globalisation is monetary. Enormous amounts of capital get allocated across national borders. Increased allocations to Europe are helping the euro to rise. The forex market is huge, with funds crossing national borders in nanoseconds, twenty four hours a day. It is still dominated by the U.S. dollar, but the euro is gaining ground and might replace the U.S. currency.

Culture is yet another form of globalisation. Bon Jovi certainly played a very important part in influencing the younger generation in the Soviet Union; cartoons from Japan are now changing the face of video games around the world. Religion and self-discipline also play a critical role in cultural globalisation.

But I believe this process would be that much slower if multiple platforms didn't carry it across national borders.

The most important platform is the language of communication. English is the de facto Esperanto of today. When the Treaty of Rome was being discussed, Europeans argued about whether the main language should be French or German or English. Nowadays so many people in Germany speak English that they have been ranked number one in English language proficiency by the United Nations, along with the Chinese.

Microsoft Windows enables us to communicate via a platform which is the de facto operating system of personal computers. The dollar is yet another very important settlement platform as well as a device to accumulate savings. VISA and Mastercard make it possible for me to shop in Berlin but settle the purchase in Tokyo. And there are many international media channels that accelerate the process of globalisation: CNN, BBC, Fox, MTV.

These platforms form the necessary basis for an emerging cyber-culture. And I think that the development of cyber-culture is helping create a novel kind of cultural diversity. We can already see its new aspects shaping up: cyber-leadership and cyber-teamwork. A new global community is being formed through e-learning, e-systems and e-business systems which are causing a very rapid change in our society. People can e-design products across cultural and national borders in a collaborative environment. Then such products can be e-manufactured, e-financed, e-sold and e-serviced.

In this new, totally different culture we have to distinguish clearly between global and domestic leadership. Take values, for example. The Americans would say: "shareholder value first". Japanese companies would say: "no, employees' interests first." A new concept would be: customers' interests first. Participatory culture and a efficient use of time are encouraged under a global leadership. When you work for a global company and a very important chief executive of a dealership dies, should you attend the funeral as far away as Japan, or should you continue to watch the World Cup? Patriotism is also an important factor, as are the existence and location of the global corporate headquarters.

We should forget all about ethnic and cultural differences, since global corporations tend to develop a different and arrogant culture – the corporate culture. This culture dictates that the orders issued by corporate headquarters are tantamount to law.

Here's an example of how modern communication functions – or, rather, malfunctions. Recently, Japan's government bonds were rated A2 by Standard & Poors, so one of its ministers – the Minister of International Trade and Industry – said that such rating had put Japan below Bosnia. He also said that in Bosnia more than 50% of the population were suffering from Aids, and that for Japan's rating to be below Bosnia's – well, someone had better examine the rating agency itself since the guys there must have been out of their minds. He said all of this at a private meeting. But this "kitchen talk" was leaked, and the media carried it all over the world, and he has been criticised and might have to resign.

Communication can function via paper, face-to-face, phone calls, close-circuit TV, voice-over-IP. The latter is done over the Internet and is beginning to be used quite widely as the cheapest form of communication. This technology is helping shape a new sort of leadership which I call "cyber-leadership". This is very different from the traditional style of leadership. When you are behind a computer keyboard, it is like being behind the steering wheel of an automobile. When you are steering a car with 120-hp engine, you become a different person. It's a wonderful environment. In such intellectual exchange logic overcomes gender, looks, age and academic record.

But while companies need to have people with cyber-leadership qualities, such leaders often have no real-life experience, so they don't know how to cope with reality. And yet this can be a very powerful tool because language and logic are critical in business, and an ability to marshal the facts is very important.

Now, many companies are trying to nurture cyber-leadership. Cisco Systems, for instance, is an almost virtual company which nevertheless employs thirty thousand people. But while this company doesn't manufacture anything itself, it is in the business of making routers. So a global community of employees participates in its open production system.

The Cisco example shows that we are migrating from a traditional business system to a web-shaped corporation, where the prototype developers would sit in Silicon Valley, software writers would work in Bangalore, manufacturing would be done in China, marketing would take place in Europe and the U.S. and money would be assembled by VISAs and Mastercards. This type of web-shaped corporation requires a very, very different style of leadership and communication. So it is fundamentally cross-cultural, cross-national and even goes beyond ethnic and cultural groups.

For a company to be successful, it has to have some form of web-shaped corporate capability. Recently, Microsoft launched Xbox, a computer-game hardware platform to compete with Sony's Play Station 2. And how in the world could a software company ship hardware products? The answer is EMS – Electronic Manufacturing System, in this case represented by a company called Flextronics in Singapore. By using such cyber-collaborators, Microsoft was able to convert itself into a manufacturing company, although it had zero experience in making any hardware.

There's another very important development underway which I call "cross-border migration of jobs". Several years ago, financial service firms started setting up shop in Dublin and taking jobs away from American companies, particularly in insurance and credit card clearance over the phone. But now the phenomenon is across the board – manufacturing, R & D, back-office and indirect work, call centres, marketing cells, logistics, finance, service, repair and maintenance.

In this way, jobs migrate world-wide over the phone and Internet. There are locations which seem to be able to attract very interesting kinds of jobs that can be done over the Web or over the phone. In Europe, for example, it's Ireland, which has by now won over quite a few American corporations as customers. On the European continent, the Netherlands has acted as a key back-office service cluster for many corporations who prefer outsourcing. India is becoming a fantastic location for back-office operations of companies like GE Capital, American Express, Amazon.com and Citicorp. China is creating a cluster for outsourced back-office services and call centres for Japan; Australia does the same for the U.S. com-panies on the Asian continent, and Singapore has become the location of choice for corporate headquarters for the South-Asian region.

This cyber-culture is emerging right in front of our eyes. This is a new globalisation of citizens: generation gap, language gap, and lifestyle gap are all being overcome. And we also see the emergence of "Nintendo kids": These are teenagers who play the same kind of games, develop the same kind of stories as they grow up, tend to think alike, act alike and even have common value systems. Business schools round the world are now dominated by two or three superstar professors who attract cyber-students on the Net, the Michael Jordans, so-to-say, of academia.

This is how more prosperous regions are borrowing from the rest of the world. Very few countries and regions have prospered because they possess rich natural resources. Wealth is shifting from nations to peripheral regions of big nations and even to individuals. When the stock market was strong, the company that Paul Allen and Bill Gates had founded, in terms of its market capitalisation, was bigger than the entire GNP of Korea.

Prosperous regions tend now to be very regional in character. Nation-states are not – but then they are also much less prosperous. And that is a huge problem for such centrally controlled nation-states as Japan or Germany. I believe that a nation-state is no longer a unit of economic prosperity. This is one of the reasons why I'm spending most of my time trying to convince the Japanese, especially politicians, to form the "Doshu Republic" of Japan, which would be a federation of autonomous regions.

Look at China: It has achieved a sea change by gradually dismantling its central control, by forming about a dozen smaller Taiwans on its coastline and de facto migrating its government structure from being centrally controlled to the United States of Chunghua which means "prosperous Chinese states". Eight of these Chunqhua regions are among the top fifteen countries in Asia that include more or less anyone who counts in Asia.

Because these regions have such autonomy and, when taken together, dwarf other Asian nations, they compete fiercely for the four "I"s that I mentioned above. Japanese electronic companies are migrating into China at a great pace, and Americans frantically import Chinese goods, making China very much a production place for everyone else. Its stock market is going up. Its capital is coming from the rest of the world.

At the same time Japanese language call centres have started appearing in former Manchuria, where about half a million people speak Japanese. Here language capability based on historical ties has made it possible for Japanese indirect services to migrate across the border to Shenyang, Dalian and other former Manchuria states. The cost of operating, for example, a call centre in China is about one-twentieth of running it in Japan.

It is becoming clear that cyber-ethnic groups are now being formed as strategic business units. Take Ireland, for instance: Its current population is only 3.5 million, but there are 70 million

Irish living outside of the country. So Irish eHubs have become a household name in the industry, as its call centres have taught us a great deal about ethnic strategic grouping in cyberspace.

To summarise, globalisation is a physical phenomenon, and companies must embrace it because such developments are irreversible. The global new economy is here to stay. Some of the companies that have taken advantage of new forces have grown ten times faster in the last ten years. Capital is migrating massively across national borders. Market capitalisation, thus engaged, is an offensive weapon, as proven by the case of AOL taking over Time Warner. Globalisation and cross-border mergers and acquisitions are a fact of life, and local success on its own is no longer sustainable.

We see how virtual single companies are being formed and how virtual cyber-ethnic groups are delivering competitive advantages. A totally different cyber-culture is challenging the corporate world in ways that override the traditional cultural and generational gaps. Managers who refuse to learn how to deal with such new challenges are doomed to fail.

# Competitive Advantage Through Diversity

## Rama Bijapurkar
Founder and Chairperson, Management Consulting, Mumbai

In the world of business, the issue of diversity is not all that complex, nor is tolerating diversity a hard thing to do, because business the world over is united by one common interest, and that is Profit. Profit and profitable growth (subject, obviously, to ethical values) is the common altar that all businesses, irrespective of nationality, worship at! And around the world, any business that fails to be profitable gets punished by the stock markets. So to that extent, we have fertile ground for tolerance of diversity. If diversity makes good economic sense, then business will and does embrace it. In the global market cyber world, diversity is largely irrelevant, because when people interact as disembodied voices or messages on a computer screen, differences don't show up easily. In the more physical world, diversity represents a huge competitive advantage, because how can a business target diverse customers, leverage the best suppliers around the world, attract international investors, sell to women, if it is not internally diverse? So the issue is not so much whether a business should be diverse, but whether it can afford not to be, because diversity is a major source of competitive advantage.

Diversity leads to more holistic problem-solving. The advantage of having someone from outside a culture take a look at a problem in another culture, or context, is that the "taken-for-granted, doesn't-everyone-know" assumptions are questioned. This leads to better quality problem-solving and, hopefully, higher economic gain. Gender diversity is another "it-makes-sense" issue. Women make up a unique segment of employees who come with distinctive price-value equations: "give me flexibility to take care of my child and I will give you my life, I will work and burn the midnight oil". If a business fails to leverage these price performance or price-value equations that are so readily available, it puts itself at a competitive disadvantage.

What can leadership do to get organisations to whole heartedly embrace diversity? Leadership can drive the "this-makes-better-business-sense" aspect of diversity strongly, make the debate within organisations rational and cognitive rather than emotional.

I want to mention a certain kind of intolerance of thought, which has been described by one of the management thinkers as "corporate imperialism". When foreign business entered the liberalized Indian market, many came with a set of tried and tested formulae that they were trying to transplant from the developed world or from experiences in other developing countries all of which they grouped into one third world whole! The result: Huge global businesses started losing money. They had to find out the hard way that the Indian market has unique demand structures. We consist of lots of people who buy little; not a few people who buy a lot. And to make money out of that situation, whether you are a retailer or a bank, requires a somewhat different approach. So foreign businesses had to be tolerant of our differences, our diversity. At the same time, we in the developing world have to be tolerant of them and accept that as long as we still have to overcome the Third World tag, even though we have a lot to offer, we have to conform first. You don't get to shape the rules until you are successful. If you have to play by the rules first in order to shape them later, that's fine.

… How do you bring about a uniform organisation culture in a very, very diverse corporation? My area of work is market strategy so I'll use global brands as an example. Global brands have to mean the same thing the world over. They don't have to be the same thing. The values have to be the same, whether it's MTV or whether it's Deutsche Bank. But the attributes may be completely different. So that, I think, is the anatomy of dealing with diversity.

# Minorities and Majorities

## Peter Goldmark
Chairman and CEO, International Herald Tribune, Paris

Diversity, tolerance – we live in a world which is becoming infinitely more sensitive to difference in ethnic culture and religion. We have left a century where most of the collisions seem to be ideological or national and we have entered a century where once again, the ethnic, the cultural, the religious, the sectarian rub a little bit more closely. What is a minority and what is a majority? Those words and concepts have no sense outside a specific context. Mathematically, you need a set, or a field, in which to have a minority or a majority. How have we human beings grown up, how have we evolved as a species? I would argue that everything we imagine and see and observe takes place in what I would call an arena of consciousness. We construct a circle of experience from our youngest days as a child, and everything that happens to us happens within that. Now, for several hundreds of thousands of years, that arena of experience was the territory of the hunter-gatherer tribe. All of our genes, all our cultural habits were formed in that context. And in that arena of consciousness, the entire human race grew up as members of a majority. You would have a territory; sometimes you would meet another group of 15 to 20 people. They would look just like your group. Once in a while you came in contact with another group at the outer limit that looked different, whose skin was a different color, or who had a different way of worshipping the gods. But most of the human race grew up adapting through natural selection to being part of a majority.

We move then to the agricultural settlements 10,000 years ago – same thing, most people looked just like you looked. Then we move to the city states, then we move to the nation state – but we are still in an arena of consciousness where most human beings grew up experiencing life as members of a majority.

But today we live in a very different way. Some time during the 20th century, most of us experienced the fact that our arena of consciousness was enlarged, by a significant measure, as in the way in which an electron "jumps" to a different ring in quantum physics. And in this "jump", what happened was that our arena of consciousness extended to the entire globe. Perhaps this began with people walking on the moon – remember those beautiful pictures of the earth from the moon? Maybe part of it was people in Mongolia watching "Dallas" on TV. We all know these stories. But we now live in a world where a large portion of the world's decision-makers and a sizeable amount of its population conceive of themselves as living on the planet as a whole. And on the planet as a whole – with the world as a whole as our arena of consciousness – for the first time in human history, we are all ethnic and religious and cultural minorities. And I believe that at a very quiet, long-wave level, this is a very powerful change. It will put a premium on something many women already know, and that many people in other parts of the world already know: namely, that the skills of the person who is a part of the minority are different from the skills of the person who is a part of the majority. Minority people learn to listen differently, they learn to pick up signs of danger differently, they watch carefully how the majority culture behaves. They possess a different set of skills that are often softer, more adaptive, more responsive, less assertive.

And we are all minorities now.

# From the One Culture Bank to the One Bank Culture

Tessen von Heydebreck

Member of the Board of Managing Directors, Deutsche Bank, Frankfurt

The Deutsche Bank is over 130 years old. In the past, we were proud of our one culture bank: we were recognised on the street and identified as typical German bankers. We exported our business culture, which had been very successful on the home market for many decades, to other countries. We filled managerial posts in these countries with people from Germany. However, over the last 25 years we have learned that we cannot conquer the world by proceeding in this way. While our business is expanding and becoming ever more diversified, we strive in the first place to be true to the principle of being one bank and one team.

This does not, however, mean that we are striving for a culture of uniformity. Quite the contrary! "One bank culture" no longer means "one culture bank". We welcome the diversity within our bank – the differences between regions, business areas, functions and people. This diversity is of definite advantage to us. Only by respecting it, valuing it and making purposeful use of it can we function efficiently.

We must also create the platform which will enable us to raise the treasure concealed within the diverse talents of our many colleagues. We must give our colleagues the opportunity to apply their manifold talents and to make their ideas count in the bank. With the foundation of the Global Diversity group, the management board has put itself at the forefront of this development. The group's motto is "Global Diversity – A Wealth of Talents". It sets the standards, recommends procedures and monitors compliance with the behaviour code that we have set up for the board.

For the Deutsche Bank, diversity is not just a short-lived trend aimed at giving particular privileges to presumed minorities. It is, on the contrary, an essential element in a future-oriented global business strategy. All our workers should have the opportunity to make creative use of the full potential of their personal abilities. Gender, ethnic origin, age, disability and sexual orientation are of no importance – the only thing that matters is if and how every individual employee contributes to the success of our bank.

The firm support for diversity in our company is not therefore simply a question of social ethics, but must above all be seen from the perspective of the positive influence it exerts on our business success. The aim is to find the best person for a real job in a real place. And so, for example, there is hardly a manager or a branch leader who is German in our foreign branches today.

In this context, let me select from a multiplicity of projects a few themes that are particularly important to us. For example, we saw the need for action on the question of women in leading positions. Over 50% of our employees are women. Three years ago, only ten to 12% of our managers were women – and we have succeeded, by the use of various measures such as mentoring, cross-mentoring and network-building, in increasing this figure to 22%. Unfortunately, it is still exceptional for a woman to have a job in the very highest echelons, but we are going to change that. Our aim is to have women in 10% of the top positions throughout the world.

By getting rid of prejudice and promoting mutual tolerance, the bank is trying to do its bit to create a positive working atmosphere. In this respect, the Rainbow Group, which is a network representing the interests of gays, lesbians, bi- and trans-sexual people in the bank, comes into play. The Rainbow Group is simultaneously a contact for target-group marketing in the business sphere, a synergy effect that has positive results, given the increasing diversity of our customer base.

Furthermore it is already becoming clear that because of demographic change the proportion of older employees in relation to younger employees is increasing, and that we must react to this. Age diversity and employability have become important strategic factors. Continuing education by know-how-transfer from older to younger employees, or a greater admixture of employees from all age groups in training provision, which will simultaneously promote competent transfer of knowledge, coaching and mentoring, are just some of the projects aimed at conserving the experience and knowledge of older employees.

We are increasingly adopting a perspective focussed on the phases of life, which includes all our employees equally.

Diversity is our opportunity. But diversity also conceals risks, problems and increased complexity. We must face up to these challenges. We do this by continually creating frameworks. Only those who are ready to contribute to the success of our firm can become employees of our bank. The common principle which binds us all together, to which each and every one of our employees must be committed, is that achievement is what counts. This is the only way that we can develop the culture of achievement that is so indispensable for our success. And only those who not only accept our company values, but also live up to them, will be able to stay with us in the long term. Our values are focus on the client, teamwork, innovation, achievement and trust. Some of these values cannot be transformed into action at all, if we do not make diversity our watchword.

We recruit our employees on the basis of their potential, not their variety. And yet the diversity in our bank guarantees the high level of creativity that will ensure our success tomorrow.

# Diversity in the Work World

## Vural Öger
Founder and Director, Öger Tours, Hamburg

In the Germany of the sixties and seventies, the idea of a homogenous German nation held sway. Since then there has been a paradigmatic change in the direction of variety in German society. In this context the new citizenship law is a very important step in the right direction.

Diversity is an invaluable source of talent, creativity and experience. Diversity increases competitiveness because it expands the potential for ideas and innovations. Mixed teams can approach problems from several directions at once because of the different cultural and social backgrounds of the players, and this makes the team more productive, and more able to find better solutions.

One of the main prerequisites for diversity is tolerance. And tolerance presupposes a learning process. Children have a way of getting together and forming friendships without prejudice. Tolerance is a vital element in the upbringing of children and in day-to-day behaviour. The development of prejudices against cultures, races and religions must be avoided at all costs.

In this way we can select what is best in various cultures and put it all together. In this process not only multinational firms, but also any small business which is limited to its own town or region, can set an example and show how much they benefit from the cultural diversity of their workforce. It is not their cultural or ethnic roots that count, but character and professional skills, as well as loyalty to the company. There is therefore no reason at all why a quarter or more of the staff in a German firm should not be of foreign origin. We have long been aware that it is not the origins of our staff but their personal commitment and abilities that are important. As businessmen, we too have a duty to communicate this knowledge to the public and the community.

# A Matter of Leadership

## Museji A. Takolia

Senior Adviser, Diversity Strategy & Equal Opportunities, Cabinet Office, Government of the United Kingdom, London

It is a self-evident truth perhaps to say that businesses do not exist in a vacuum. Employers are, by necessity, limited instruments for the implementation of social policy. For Governments there are however issues to address and be seen to lead on. For us social policy is a primary purpose, a place from where we aim to be at the vanguard of developments on issues like diversity in the workplace.

There is a societal context too for business, a fact that explains why so many of us see business and social issues as hand-in-hand. It is one of the reasons why leading companies drive ahead with an agenda for corporate social responsibility.

This is all right and proper, but the truth is that rights in the workplace have had to be fought for, so governments have over time, intervened with legislation. We know from our experience in the UK that labour markets are stubborn; it takes time for change to take root. Despite having a better educated workforce, some employers continue to behave irrationally; they continue to discriminate against minorities and women. This has little to do with the qualification or ability of the people coming forward. Selection is on the basis of different, irrational and unfair criteria. This is why leadership strategies need to start by supporting legislation to protect workers from unlawful discrimination at work and in wider society. Here in Europe, provisions in the European Convention on Human Rights and the European Employment Framework Directive will provide further redress against other forms of discrimination in the workplace e.g. age, religion and sexuality. However, there are few places in the world where legislative provisions alone have captured the entirety of the problems they seek to address.

I am in the Cabinet Office of the British Government as the Senior Adviser on Diversity Strategy & Equal Opportunities. As a leading public sector organisation with around 150 different government departments and agencies and c.480,000 employees, it is my job to make sure that the process of modernisation and reform impacts on the diversity of the civil service, or rather, that diversity in both employment and services is a necessary part of the modernisation and reform agenda. In my own organisation, the British Civil Service, we have gone beyond protecting employees by implementing minimal legislative protection. We have taken positive action by setting a target for a fair and balanced representation of women, ethnic minorities and disabled employees among our c.3,300 senior civil servants. We aim to have 35% of our senior civil service (SCS) made up of women by 2004/5. At present, women make up half of our total workforce, but at last count in October 2001, 24% of our senior civil servants were women. We have similarly set targets to double the number of ethnic minority and disabled employees to 3.2% and 3.0% of the SCS respectively.

On the other hand, I do believe there is a balance in all this vis-à-vis our roles as employers. In our case the Government or other public bodies can set expectations, but as employers, we are and will always be limited instruments of social policy. Today, businesses, whether public serving public goals or in the private sector with more commercial objectives in mind, are acting out of enlightened self-interest. The credibility and effectiveness of what they do is now defined by diversity as a business imperative.

Company boards, the heterogeneous teams that serve companies, are delivering services to an increasingly informed and diverse population. Another self-evident truth: diversity is no longer a choice. Companies that approach diversity as a bolt-on will produce bolt-on results; be it as an employer or one in search of commercial goals in mixed and diverse markets.

The world I live and work in has changed in other ways. It is no longer about bad people saying and doing bad things. In Europe and particularly in Britain we have highly effective legislation to deal with direct discrimination in the workplace. The more difficult issue for us to deal with is one of good people doing good things and who still produce a culture in the workplace that amounts to "institutionalised discrimination". Institutionalised discrimination is the product of policies, procedures, practices and behaviours that are in themselves benign, but that have the effect of producing barriers for example, to the recruitment and advancement of women, of black people, of disabled people. In this scenario therefore, the solutions lie in management – diversity then is about general management. It's just about good management. The prism of equality and fairness simply exposes the fault lines. These fault lines run deeper than we like to think, and go beyond the issues of under-representation.

I conclude the points I wish to introduce in this discussion by saying that leadership is vital. I recently commissioned research which took evidence from 140 U.K. employees, some globally based, all interested in bringing about a difference in the workforce. It became clear that the number one priority for leaders in the private and public sector was visible and sustained leadership on diversity. Change, whether in public or private sector organisations, is driven by leaders with a clear sense of their corporate social responsibility. In the private sector this responsibility enables a company to realise the opportunity and respond to the reality of the commercial world, that diversity has a commercial reality. It also makes it possible to implement diversity through business planning, thereby strengthening the business case. In organisations with a high performance driven culture, there is then a strong connection between diversity and accountability for performance through the business planning/objective and target setting process.

# Paul S. Miller

Commissioner, U.S. Equal Employment Opportunity Commission, Washington D.C.

# Diversity and Tolerance in the Work Environment

We are living in troubled times. In the United States, we are now wondering how to achieve the twin values of tolerance and diversity in an insecure, post-September 11th world. Security concerns should not overwhelm these values; indeed, it is more important than ever that they be integrated into our economic, social and political life. The world is shrinking and becoming more complex, and we must explore ways to understand and accept difference.

For years now, America has been trying to figure out how to deal with the problem of discrimination and the barriers in employment that deny people opportunity. Sadly, however, fears, myths, stereotypes, biases, and bigotries continue to interfere with workplace decision-making. Business suffers as a result, because it is not able to benefit fully from the unique qualities and skills of every potential worker. I believe that no economy can afford to waste a single person.

The causes, effects and consequences of discrimination within the public sector are no less significant than within the private sector. If anything, the need for diversity in public institutions is greater. Are not governmental solutions to society's ills better conceived and carried out when developed by a civil service that is a true cross-section of the people? Will not a policy option achieve increased acceptance when all with a stake in the outcome have had an opportunity to participate and to be heard? Should not legal determinations be made by judges with diverse backgrounds and educations and experiences reflecting both the breadth and the depth of the society in whose name they pass judgment?

Anti-discrimination laws and diversity programs exist to help make the workplace more fair and more just. However, the issue is complicated by the fact that such programs must operate within a context of sensitivity to the rights of groups who have traditionally benefited from the inequities.

The demographics of the workplace in the United States (U.S.), and indeed across the globe, have shifted dramatically. The U.S. Census Bureau estimates that by the middle of this new century, racial minorities will make up almost half the U.S. population. In California, the most populous state in the U.S., Americans of European background are already in the minority, and by 2015, more than 50% of the population of Texas will be minority. The integration of the countries of the European Union (E.U.), with the near-elimination of borders for E.U. citizens, means that European nations will be subject to shifting populations on a scale never before contemplated. Moreover, technology has shrunk the size of the world. It is quite clear that employers, both public and private, have an inherent interest in understanding and responding to increasing diversity in their applicant pool, workforce, and customer base.

Today, we live in a multi-cultural, multi-racial, multi-ethnic, and multi-religious global village, and the micro-communities we inhabit are becoming more multi by the day. Each of our populations reflect this new reality. The workplace is the environment where, as we say in America, the rubber hits the road, for it mirrors this growing diversity. Now more than ever, people of different backgrounds, races, ethnicities, religious practices, are obliged to interact on the job and in commerce. Managers and co-workers must learn to accept and embrace diversity, rather than alienate those who are different. Diversity in the workplace can be a means to reduce prejudice and achieve greater tolerance and understanding among people of different backgrounds and experiences.

Hostility to immigrants cannot exist in our ever-shrinking world. Intolerance can never be legitimate.

Czech President Vaclav Havel has stated, "Differences between cultures or spheres of civilization should be interpreted as an impulse to promote better knowledge of one another, more profound understanding and greater mutual respect, and not as a reason for enmity or even as a pretext for confrontation."

However, a focus on diversity solely in terms of race or ethnic origin is too narrow. This is because there are others in society who also face bias and stereotyping which prevent them from achieving full potential in the workplace.

Civil rights can no longer be defined as simply the fight against racism or gender stereotyping. Today, civil rights and diversity must also include issues affecting ethnic and language minorities, religious minorities, the elderly, people with disabilities, gays and lesbians. I believe that the greatest single legacy of the American civil rights experience has been the gradual expansion of legal protections to a broad range of disenfranchised groups within society, thereby creating a stronger and more diversely talented workforce on all levels.

Justin Dart, the father of the international disability civil rights movement, once said, "Our [American] forefathers and mothers came to this country because we offered unique legal guarantees of equal opportunity. They got rich, and America got rich. Every time we expanded our civil rights guarantees to include another oppressed minority, America got richer. America is not rich in spite of civil rights. America is rich because of civil rights."

What has sparked the American movement towards inclusion? I believe it stems from a growing recognition that civil rights are concerned with more than our immutable characteristics, such as race and gender. At a basic level, civil rights are simply about treating people with the dignity and respect they are due as human beings, and removing arbitrary barriers in society that impede people from seeking their full potential.

As a Commissioner of the U.S. Equal Employment Opportunity Commission (EEOC), I am charged with overseeing the enforcement of all employment discrimination statutes in both the public and private sectors. My daily work is about regulating and responding to discrimination in the workplace.

I do not believe that simply championing non-discrimination as a worthy goal will create change. The genuine desire for diversity must be supported by a fair and credible system of legal enforcement. Otherwise, institutions will not change, bad actors will have no deterrent, and disenfranchised individuals will not even expect fairness. While I recognize that not every country shares the same love for litigation as does the United States, I still

believe that some degree of legal enforcement with serious penalties for violations are important to remove biases and increase diversity.

As the great American civil rights leader, Martin Luther King Jr., so aptly concluded, "Morals cannot be legislated, but behavior can be regulated. The law cannot make an employer love me, but it can keep him from refusing to hire me because of the color of my skin."

And yet, a purely legal approach to diversity has its own shortfalls. While most people of good will recognize the ultimate benefits of even-handed treatment, many worry that simply mandating equality, even with legal penalties, will not erase the disadvantages imposed by centuries of prejudice and deprivation. U.S.

President Lyndon Johnson suggested nearly forty years ago, that there is a lot of catching up to do: "You do not take a person who, for years, has been hobbled by chains and liberate him, bring him up to the starting line in a race and then say, 'you are free to compete with all the others,' and still justly believe that you have been completely fair."

In America, policies of affirmative action have played a critical role in integrating American society and ensuring that the nation's best and brightest have the opportunity to demonstrate their abilities and contribute to the economic and social life of our nation. Affirmative action is not about the inclusion of unqualified people. It is about expanding the pool of candidates that will be taken into consideration. It is about considering whether and how qualified persons of diverse backgrounds can contribute to a learning experience or to the cultivation of additional markets in an increasingly global economy. Recruiting people who have been traditionally excluded and who are qualified is simply good business because their diverse viewpoints mirror the diversity of our world.

Disabled people are one of the least politically powerful groups in society. Nevertheless, opportunities for disabled people are slowly opening up in the United States, in large part due to the recent passage of the Americans with Disabilities Act (ADA). The ADA is a simple but revolutionary new law. Simple, because the purpose of the law is to outlaw discrimination against disabled people. The ADA seeks to ensure that persons with disabilities are integrated into mainstream economic and social life, and that this integration occurs without paternalism. Revolutionary, because it requires employers to make reasonable accommodations or adjustments to enable disabled workers to compete for, and succeed in, jobs. The law creates an affirmative duty to take into account a worker's disability as long as such an accommodation does not create an undue hardship. Moreover, the law sets standards of architectural access for people with disabilities to businesses, shops, hotels, restaurants and to public transit systems. The law has served as a vehicle of historic change for disabled people, and any discussion of diversity and tolerance must recognize that attitudes about, and fears of, disabled people must continue to change in order that this community take its rightful place at society's table.

While I believe that this creative ferment will ultimately lead to a commonly shared vision of humanity, the reality is that work place decisions are not made in a vacuum. They are made both for reasons of merit and on personal grounds. And it is this personal dimension that is often influenced by bias.

As a law student at the Harvard Law School, I found that the very law firms that had pursued me based on my résumé would immediately lose all interest in employing me as soon as they met me or learned of my size. In fact, I was told by one law firm that even though they personally had no problem with my size, they feared that their clients would think that they were running – and here I quote what they told me – "a circus freak show" if their clients were to see me as a lawyer in their firm.

At that time, before the passage of the ADA, such behavior did not yet violate federal statute, and persons subjected to such blatant discriminatory behavior had no recourse. This experience left me with a deep and personal understanding of the urgent necessity for civil rights protection in the workplace. It is this experience that makes me better able to empathize with the types of issues that I confront as Commissioner of the EEOC. I know how it feels to be trapped in someone else's stereotype, and to be denied opportunities based upon bigotry. It doesn't feel good. It's not fair. It's not right. And it must not be tolerated in any workplace.

Learning and working in a diverse environment are important because, in the words of former Texas governor Ann Richards, "the perspective is different. The experience is different. The knowing is different." A classroom discussion about sexual harassment is different when both men and women are in the room. A debate about healthcare reform is different when a person with a disability is in the room. A policy discussion about immigration is different when ethnic minorities are in the room. A corporate marketing meeting is different when racial minorities are in the room. The end product is better because it includes input from different perspectives and experiences. And I believe that is true whether you are talking about a university classroom, a policy discussion in government, or a strategy discussion in a corporation. After all, customers, clients and citizens all reflect this same diversity.

The challenge of achieving diversity within an organization is not easy. It requires you to examine your own biases and assumptions made about people who are different from yourself. Even well-meaning people may harbor views that unfairly limit individuals in subtle or paternalistic ways. For example, one might refuse to promote a woman because of concerns that she might plan on having children, requiring an absence during a maternity leave; one might fail to hire a qualified blind person for a job because of unsubstantiated fears regarding his ability to get to work on time; a company might choose to hold a reception at a club that does not accept Blacks as members. Such biases may be no less limiting than overt bigotry.

Diversity requires doing things differently and affirmatively. Mentoring and management training programs, thinking broadly about your applicant and promotability pools, disseminating and enforcing a zero tolerance policy for discrimination, training supervisors in equal employment opportunity and diversity, are just some of the ways to achieve a diverse workforce. As with anything else, leadership must be clearly expressed from the top, and individuals throughout the organization must be trained and their efforts reinforced in order to achieve the goals.

In one of the last speeches of his life, the late U.S. Supreme Court Justice Thurgood Marshall challenged his audience with powerful words which remain relevant and appropriate today: "I wish I could say that racism and prejudice were only distant memories... and that liberty and equality were just around the bend. I wish I could say that America has come to appreciate diversity and to see and accept similarity. But as I look around... [people] have given up on integration and lost hope in equality...

We cannot play ostrich. Democracy cannot flourish amid fear. Liberty cannot bloom amid hate. Justice cannot take root amid rage. We must go against the prevailing wind. We must dissent from indifference. We must dissent from apathy... We must dissent because America can do better, because America has no choice but to do better."

In today's shrinking global environment, Justice Marshall's challenge to America can be equally applied to the world community. Diversity is about preserving individual dignity. It is about ensuring that employers, businesses, and public accommodations look at an individual's ability, free from stereotypes, biases or preconceived notions made about that person due to race or gender or ethnicity or religion or age or disability or sexual orientation. The challenge is to help our communities grow by fostering a spirit of inclusion and purpose that welcomes all of us. This is what I believe must be the commitment of the business community, governmental institutions, educational institutions, and this is what I believe must be the commitment of all of us, no matter what we do or where we live.

Peter Scholl-Latour, Roger van Boxtel,
Wolfgang Schäuble, Martin Schulze (moderator),
Daniel Libeskind, Gianni Vattimo

# Full Boats Now – Empty Cupboards later?

*Migration, immigration and integration have become urgent global issues. The citizens of the world are on the move, but all too often they are the needy, unskilled citizens that most countries don't want. However, the population of many prosperous countries is shrinking and, in the long run, these countries need low as well as high-skill workforce reinforcement to maintain their standard of living. Who is responsible for integrating whom? Is there any best way to resolve the dilemma and ensure intra-national tolerance?*

# A Hypocritical Discussion

Roger van Boxtel

Minister for Urban Policy and Integration of Ethnic Minorities, The Hague

It may well be that when a country such as the Netherlands is prospering, it witnesses an increase in xenophobia. There was a time when we needed more workers – that is no longer the case. Unemployment is very low – around 3%. Even among the minorities in the country, unemployment has dropped from 16% only a few years ago to a present 9%. Nevertheless, Mr. Fortuyn was a clever politician. He was able to tap a reservoir of resentment, especially among the young. He attacked integration, he claimed the boat was already too full. But what exacerbated the situation was September 11th. Many of the immigrants to the Netherlands over the past ten years are Muslims. The culture they have brought with them is different from that of the immigrants from the former Dutch colonies, from the Mediterranean countries. This has caused considerable change. But nobody ever comes up with the idea that it would be good if people got together and talked to each other.

…I find the discussion about integration hypocritical. Elite and hypocritical. Why don't we talk more about development aid? How much is Europe paying to the countries where all the people come from? Practically nothing. The Netherlands contributes 1% of its Gross National Product. So does Denmark. Many of the other countries of Europe contribute less than half a percent. We are also hypocritical in our claim that we need workers to guarantee our future, that Europe needs to develop both an immigration and an integration policy. What we see, however, is that Europe is unable to come up with either. It produces beautiful words but no action. Nothing happens. So eventually, Italy, Spain, Germany and Holland will be competitors on the labour market, we'll all be searching for people. As for integration, how are we going to manage that? Many of the immigrants come to our countries hardly knowing their own national language, never mind a European lingua franca. No wonder that they look for familiarity within their own community.

…In Holland, we are investing a tremendous amount of money in teaching people Dutch, in teaching them what the rules and regulations are in our country, not because we want to assimilate the newcomers, but because we want to integrate them. We are spending over 200 million euro per year in these programs, whereas Germany, so very much larger than Holland, is spending a mere 50 million euro per year. To integrate people, a country needs to invest in them. I think that the rest of Europe should learn from what we are doing and adopt similar policies.

…Another problem deserves mention. We still talk about a multicultural society but, in fact, what people experience is a multi-individual society, and that is very bad. There is no cohesion between groups any longer. Majorities are affected too, because they are not majorities any longer, they are becoming minorities. The same seems to be happening in Germany. And to manage that process is the biggest political challenge we have to confront.

…Everybody in a position of responsibility has to work at reducing fear. We just have to consider the escalating madness in the relationship between the West and the Muslim countries. That madness is being fed from all sides. Recently in the Netherlands, we had a tremendous uproar because 5 radical Imams preached in the Mosque that we should pray for the martyrs who did such a great job in the September 11$^{th}$ attack. And they demanded gardens for Muslim women, so that they don't have to go out into the streets, and don't have to work in the supermarkets. And that was shown on television.

# The Beauty of Integration

## Daniel Libeskind
Architect, Berlin

I've been an immigrant and an emigrant all my life. I was born a Jew in Poland, I went to Israel, I lived in New York, now I'm in Berlin. I think we are looking at immigration the wrong way.

I think we should openly recognize (society's) need for strangers, the need for people who are different, without making a distinction between political and economic migrants. We should not ask, "where have you come from?" but "where you are going?" That is what America does and that is the strength of America. And I think the paranoia, the obsession about identity, the notion that we really belong somewhere, are false. Because, in the end, where do we all come from? Who gave us a stake in a particular place? I am not happy with a global agoraphobia and paranoia about the world.

...Integration is a word, a piece of grammar, that one has to address because integration is usually the idea that other people will become like you are. But the beauty of integration in the true sense is that it allows identity and difference to coexist. When I was in Los Angeles recently, I went to McDonalds and the young woman there spoke Chinese, not a word of English. Then I went to do my laundry. Somebody spoke Spanish, not a word of English. Then I went to a restaurant. Somebody spoke Afghani, not a word... and I thought, what a beautiful country, where people don't have to speak English. They can speak Yiddish, they can speak Polish, and yet they can fight back, and find a way of going ahead. So I think the idea of integration, of thinking of the borders, of quantifying statistically, calculating what is a good order for Europe, is missing the point. Because I think Europe is a spiritual idea. And a spiritual idea is not just a linguistic idea. And I think that a lot of the debates about integration really just mask the fact that in schools the way foreigners are seen is already distorted by ideologies which are hardly relevant to today's world.

...I have just returned from Toronto, where there are 160 languages, foreign languages, taught in schools. Public schools in Toronto teach 160 different languages, up to a certain grade, with English as a second language. And I don't think that these people are going to wind up in the service industries, this is a highly-educated class which is actually given a chance in the world to be themselves and also to be part of the world.

...But where is the irritation (about immigration) coming from? The irritation comes from the overall notion of a certain homogenous world which denies the plurality and the globality of interrelationships. I really don't like the idea of a world defined by an elite. I think people have been underestimated, because people have not really been given the opportunity to speak about, and interact with, something other than just political notions of economy and making money and succeeding in the future.

...I don't think it matters whether you're a Christian or a Jew or a Muslim – I think the problem of tolerance should go beyond the discussion of a material world. The human structure, the human world and the revolution of the human world are never made just on a material level. It's always connected to what people think the world is about, where they are, what is home and what is homelessness, what is security and the ultimate lack of security which human beings have been exposed to in their own lives.

(Tolerance) is not a problem of elitism, it is a problem of communication and the the fact that security has never been part of the human condition, that home has never been defined as a border that can be defended. So the problem is no longer just a European, American, Chinese, or whatever, problem, it is a global problem, and I think we are all part of the full boat. I think the full boat is not the boat coming to Germany or to America. The full boat is the world. And the empty cupboard is also the world.

# The Need for Better Integration

## Wolfgang Schäuble
MP, CDU, Former Federal Minister, Berlin

In my understanding of the term, Germany is not a country of immigration – but not because immigration does not happen. The difference is that countries of immigration determine that within a specific period of time they will accept a given number of people chosen by themselves: this process does not occur in Germany.

I am in no way opposed to immigration, but rather in favour of openness, new ideas and exchange. Nonetheless, we are deceiving ourselves if we believe that we can solve all our own development problems by means of immigration. Immigration can never be the panacea that will cure the pains caused by our own mistakes and failures.

The answer is not a matter of exclusion or selection, but of improved integration. We must win over the population at large to the idea of integration so that they are not afraid of being caught up in developments where they lose all security and sense of direction. The second and third generations of a large proportion of the people who came to Germany from Turkey have in the meantime become well integrated in Germany. But further integration is still necessary and must be brought about to such a degree that it is acceptable to the public as a whole. Integration must take place in such a way that we do not compartmentalise ourselves into separate societies and become divided from each other. This cannot be allowed to happen in an area as densely populated as Germany.

Nor can we accept a situation like that of the United States – and to some extent our own – where immigrants stick together, speak only their own mother-tongue and are recruited for particular sectors of employment which the native population does not wish to do. If this happens, we will have to admit that we have not developed very much further than the slave societies of the past.

There are also considerable problems at the other end of the scale. Thus it is, for example, an extremely dubious undertaking when we recruit talent from the computer industry in India because we can no longer fulfil the demands of the modern world for ourselves. In this way we create a brain drain without concerning ourselves about how the gap thus created can be filled in India. It is therefore not just a matter of dealing with the problems of immigration, but of asking ourselves why more people wish to leave their home countries than is good for those countries. What is absolutely necessary is to investigate the causes of this great migration and to find an appropriate way to combat them.

# Mass Migration in an Age of Bad Conscience

## Peter Scholl-Latour
Author and Journalist, Paris

There appears to be a widely held view in this country that tolerance and integration are matters that are under our control. What we are not aware of, however, is that we are living through a period of mass migration. There have always been such eras throughout history: from places where there was over-population and poverty people moved into countries which were rich and relatively sparsely populated. For example, the Roman Empire was not overthrown, it was overrun. A similar process is in train at the moment. We will not be able to halt it.

Large scale assimilation has also taken place on many occasions, as it did in Southern France, which experienced heavy Italian immigration around 1900. At the beginning, people found it hard to get on with one another, but since then the former Italians have become far better integrated in France than have the Corsicans. We can observe the same phenomenon among the Poles who came to the Ruhr area. In my childhood, processions with prayers in Polish were by no means a rarity. We will not see such things nowadays, since the former Poles have in the meantime become totally integrated and assimilated. By the way, football played a very important role in this process.

There are groups of immigrants living in Germany today, among whom we find major cultural differences. We cannot and should not ride roughshod over these differences. The "average Turk" lives here with his Turkish ideas, his religion and his own way of looking at the world, and we will not be able to take these basic bulwarks of his life away from him. Nor should we do so. But the problem is more serious. In frequent conversations with more or less fundamentalist Turks, I always say to them directly that the Crusaders and Saladin's warriors were closer to one another in many respects than Western secular society and Islamic society are today. There is no point in pretending that there is harmony where it does not exist. Fundamental differences between cultures cannot simply be glossed over.

There are guest workers, migrants and immigrants in other parts of the world as well. In the Emirates, two thirds of the population are immigrants. Let us not beat about the bush: these people are treated like dogs. Even in Turkey it was the Pakistanis who were made to do the menial work, until one day the Turks noticed that there were too many Pakistanis and expelled them overnight.

In comparison with this, European societies are exceedingly tolerant. And yet we still run around the whole time with a bad conscience – we are obviously suffering from a peculiarly European form of masochism.

# Bel Paese Between Natural Disaster and Control

## Gianni Vattimo
MEP, Party of European Socialists, Strasbourg/Brussels

Migration to Italy is a reality, a fact. Even if we wanted to, we could not keep immigrants out. So, our problem is to find a way to cope with migration. And, if you look at the statistics, Italy does not have that many immigrants, many less percentage-wise than in Germany or in France. The immigration problem in Italy is cultural, not economic. Because in the Northeast, for instance, where the Lega Nord is very popular, immigrants are needed as a workforce, but at the same time, they are demonized. This is a contradiction which can only be explained by cultural backwardness. I think resistance to immigration has to do with the Italian family tradition. It seems to be a middle and lower class phenomenon rather than an elite one. (We should not forget that Italy is also the country of the Mafia, and the Mafia is a great "family".) This family tradition may be changeable; in the meantime what we can do, and I say this as a philosopher rather than as a politician, is criticise strongly the idea of cultural identity. Because in a global world such as ours, people tend to have agoraphobic, neurotic reactions – they find refuge in their cultural, regional identity.

…The Italians recognise that they need immigrants to bolster the work force. We have calculated that without the immigrants, in the next 20 or 30 years we could no longer afford retirement benefits. Part of the problem lies in the fact that immigration has never been explicitly regulated, it has simply happened in the course of history. Great migrations of people have always been a sort of natural catastrophe. This is true of the whole of Europe. States have historically come through force, through war, through conquests by other states. Now, for the first time, we are trying to organise a union of states on the basis of democratic discussion.

…We have to organise immigration, we cannot continue to treat it as a natural catastrophe against which we have to construct barriers, frontiers, blocks. And controlled migration is possible in practice. We can negotiate with the countries of origin so that they control emigration while we help their local economy to develop. We can provide needed immigrants with professional training, linguistic training. But for ideological reasons, this is not what is happening in Europe today.

…I am in favour of Europe with open borders. It is a safer place to be. We gain nothing by prohibitionism, e.g. we simply increase the prices of drugs or encourage human trafficking. There is a lot of money to be made in transporting migrants clandestinely and illegally. We would probably end up spending a lot less if we helped poor countries get on their feet and made them more attractive to their peoples rather than try to protect ourselves against tides of immigrants. We don't invest enough to protect ourselves from this danger. Instead, we use demagogic measures to enforce zero tolerance, but this doesn't work.

…Our problem with immigrants is a cultural one, not one of race, nationality, or origins. It is therefore a problem of schooling, a problem of instruction, a problem of education. The problem is not the relationship between US and THEM, but between groups, different cultures, different communities, different languages within the same language.

Jeffrey Abramson, Barry Steinhardt, Peter Eigen, Natan Sznaider (moderator), Ilija Trojanow, Richard Goldstone, Ian Buruma

# The Intervention Conundrum

*Tolerance is also an international issue. Colonialism is dead, self-determination is the name of the game. Nations are supposedly free to choose their own ways, politically, religiously, economically... But what if the outside world considers that in doing things its own way, a particular sovereign state is violating universal human rights? Or being corrupt? Who is to decide? And at what point is it legitimate for states to "refuse to tolerate" the ways of other states and try to intervene?*

# The War of Values

## Ian Buruma
Journalist and Author, London

Tariq Ali once coined the phrase "the anti-imperialism of fools" and he was referring to the enthusiasm of certain leftists in the West who applauded Ayatollah Khomeini's revolution in Iran as something particularly grand. I think what he was really talking about is something that used to be known as "third-worldism", that is, the tendency of some western intellectuals and leftists and public commentators to see as heroes dictators in the non-western world who pose as defenders of local autonomy and self-sufficiency against western imperialism. Perhaps this explains the initial support of some intellectuals in the West for Pol Pot, Maoism and the like. This belongs to an old discussion of the local and the universal. The local is usually unique, and refers to something which the Germans once called *Kultur*, others called organic, and was in any case associated with the natural order of things. The universal, of course, stems from the ideas of the Enlightenment, and is often seen by its enemies as somehow artificial, constructed, rationalist. The idea of universalism in politics became current after the ascendancy of the United States. It was a way for the United States to link itself culturally and politically to the Old World, to Europe, where civilisation laid claim to universal, enlightened ideas as the basis for reason, for science.

Capitalism and democracy are usually claimed by their proponents to be part of civilisation and not of *Kultur*. The "third-worldists", on the other hand, see the spread or the promotion of capitalism and democracy as imperialist, that is to say, imposed by Anglo-American capitalism, by the United States, by the elders of Zion, or the like. It was summed up very nicely in a banner displayed during an anti-globalisation demonstration in Berlin: "Civilisation is Genocide".

It has become fashionable in Washington recently, after many years of rather restrained foreign policy, to reclaim universalism as an instrument or a goal of American foreign policy. The argument is that American principles are universal, and America should be prepared again to use its military force to bring civilisation, enlightenment and freedom to the benighted world. Obviously, you do not have to be a leftist to see that such claims may come with a degree of bad faith and self-serving arguments. When great powers decide what their interests are, they often use brutal means to make sure the rest of the world shares their views, and the propaganda that they are spreading freedom is not always convincing. Nonetheless, as a child of the Enlightenment, I would argue that democracy can be defended as a universal principle, or at least as a system that can be universally applied. This, however, does not mean that we have to ignore the question of culture and the local. When de Toqueville analysed American democracy in the mid-19th century, America then being a uniquely free society, he laid great store by culture and local traditions. As an explanation for a democratic system, he claimed that laws were more important than physical causes for producing a democracy, but that mores, traditions, customs were more important than laws. Being a good Catholic, a French aristocrat, he thought that organised religion was extremely important. And indeed, he argued that

American democracy would never be able to maintain itself with any degree of stability without what he described as the decency, and indeed conformism, of the New Englanders. In other words, he thought that culture was vital to democracy. He did, of course, firmly believe that the spiritual authority of organised religion should be kept rigidly separate from the secular authority of the state: if priests were to behave like politicians and politicians like priests, the system would quickly fall apart. And I think de Toqueville might have been rather shocked by some of the statements made by certain members of the United States administration, particularly Attorney General Ashcroft. I doubt if he would recognise the America of today, an America which in some respects is far less liberal than it was in the mid-19th century.

If culture has this important role to play, what about values and traditions in the non-western world, or even in the western world, where democracy does not have a traditional role? Do we say that these countries do not deserve democracy or cannot have democracy? What about the minorities in our own midst, minorities which do not have democracy as part of their cultural tradition – do we kick them out, do we change their behaviour? One particularly challenging part of the world with regard to values is Asia. Lee Kuan Yew of Singapore, Prime Minister Mahathir Mohamad of Malaysia, are particularly vociferous in claiming that democracy is a western idea that does not apply to Asians. Asian values are different and Asians therefore need more authoritarian forms of government.

I find this argumentation highly suspect, partly because values are often used by politicians to blow smoke in our eyes and justify their own monopoly on power. Moreover, when people talk about Asian values, what are they really talking about? They usually come up with vague statements about hard work, family-values that any Victorian in 19th century Britain would have come up with too. And, indeed, if you look at the values that Lee Kuan Yew calls Asian, you find that to a great extent they reflect the colonial education he received under the British. When he talks about discipline and the need for people to be educated much further to be able to cope with democracy, he is parroting the British teachers of his own colonial education. He is one of the last paragons, I would say, of British imperialism. So I think that Asian values can be dismissed, and I think that values as a whole should be dropped from the discourse of politics, at least in the case of democracy. If one thinks that democracy is, indeed, simply a Western value, part of Western mores and tradition, we would indeed be arrogant to insist that it should be applied everywhere. This would be another form of imperialism.

If, on the other hand, you simply see democracy as a good idea, the best way for government by popular consent to ensure legally guaranteed free speech, to give people the right to elect or kick out their chosen representatives in government, then, democracy becomes a very different matter. Culture, mores and values become rather irrelevant. Or at least European values become irrelevant. De Toqueville's observations, on the other hand, remain relevant because it does not matter whether you are a Muslim, a Jew or a Christian in a democracy, as long as church and

state are strictly separated. What de Toqueville considered important about mores is that they temper human behaviour, individual behaviour, and thus help maintain stability under an open system. Religion – whichever religion a person practices – is unimportant for de Toqueville's formula to work. I think this applies equally to minorities in our midst. It does not matter whether they are Muslims, Jews or Christians – just as long as the priests don't become politicians and the politicians don't become priests, the democratic system can work perfectly well. Only the enemies of democracy, political or religious, believe that spiritual life, political life, economic life and cultural life should be one indistinguishable whole. These advocates are not defending culture, they are defending their own monopoly and power.

A major dilemma concerns the Muslim minorities in the West, where certain religious leaders claim that, traditionally, there is no distinction between secular and religious authority. In fact, in much of Muslim history this was not true, and there was effectively a separation of secular and religious authority. So it would hardly require a great cultural change to say that Muslims who live in the West should accept the separation between spiritual and religious authority. The Iranian revolution was really a modern innovation and the ideology of the Iranian revolution was really created to justify the total power of the clerics. And I think anything the West can do to break such monopolies, wherever in the world, through economic, diplomatic or even, if necessary, military means, is surely a good thing. If that is globalisation or imperialism, then I am for it.

# To Intervene or Not to Intervene...

## Jeffrey Abramson
Louis Stulberg Professor of Law and Politics, Brandeis University, Boston

On the topic of tolerance and international humanitarian interventions: I think, as a general rule, we do defer to nation-states to enforce rights within their borders and to defend rights of self-determination of their people. But we are all very well aware that there are terrible, brutal exceptions to the ability of nation-states to defend equally and indiscriminately the rights of all residents. Consider that international organizations did very little in Cambodia, though everyone knew what was going on. Consider the tragically belated humanitarian responses to the killings in Rwanda, and I hardly need to belabour the point that the world needs, in the name of tolerance, in the name of universal human rights, to develop a more enforceable regime of international, legal humanitarian interventions.

... First-world countries have no right to dictate to other countries how they should live. However, circumstances arise, in my judgement far too frequently, where the reasons for intervention are precisely to buttress, to support, to under-gird the self-help forces within the Third World countries. So the question is, whether the outside intervention is undermining the possibilities of self-help in a paternalistic way, or whether it is freeing the democratic self-help forces in a particular area from an oppressive regime. That would be my criterion for intervention. Now, major powers like the United States clearly have mixed motives. I don't expect the world to be pure, but I do expect the world to be able to recognise the difference between oppressive and non-oppressive regimes, and not to hide behind a kind of cultural relativism as if violence, evil and oppression did not occur in the world.

When I arrived in Berlin recently, I wandered through Humboldt University, and read the great Karl Marx phrase, "Hitherto philosophers have merely interpreted the world, the point is to change it." Terrible things happen in the world, and we desperately need to discuss why the rest of the world still, out of a legalist paradigm, does not try to robustly define what the moral superiority of democracy is, and to stand up for certain basic human rights.

… I was asked to comment on famine relief, and I will confine myself to a personal anecdote. In 1972 I found myself living in India. By happenstance, I signed on to do famine relief in newly-established Bangladesh, primarily because I knew how to pilot ships in inland waterways. I knew nothing about famine relief. I certainly did not know that the children who came aboard the boat with bloated stomachs were, in fact, starving to death. I had just witnessed a mixed-motive intervention by India. India certainly had less than humanitarian reasons for wanting to smash Pakistan and invade in the civil war, but the fact of the matter is, the need for an intervention to save lives was clear. Now what the UN did was strike what, to my mind, was a crazy kind of deal. I had plenty of grain to deliver. I had an abundance of grain. But the causes of famine are political. Because of some bizarre notion of boundaries and state sovereignty, my authority was limited to plying the inland waterways, so that I could move grain from Chittagong to Khulna. That's what I could do. And we would unload the grain at Khulna and children would come and sweep up, from the keel of the ship, whatever grain we had spilled, presumably because they weren't getting any of it. And the reason they weren't getting any of the grain was because, though Bangladesh, as a fledgling state, did not have the capacity, there was this notion that Bangladesh should be in charge of delivering the grain by land. And this crazy deal that the UN struck meant that all of the international relief operations simply put grain into ports, moved it from port to port.

I was 19 years old at the time, I was ill-equipped to understand what it was about a world order that decreed that saving children from starving was not a moral priority. Still today, it strikes me that certain stances should be imperative upon us, should require us to take a firm stance in defense of basic human rights wherever they are violated. It should not be that hard to follow the good side of the Marx quote, that the time has long since come to change the world in the basic senses I've just been trying to identify.

# Zero Tolerance

## Peter Eigen

Founder and Chairman of the Board, Transparency International, Berlin

I wish to make a plea for zero tolerance of corruption. I would like to explode the myth which is prevalent in a great many countries, most of them rich, that corruption belongs to the value system, belongs to the morals of many (foreign) cultures, and therefore, if you step outside your own home market, you have to play the game as it is played in these other parts of the world. And I would like to vigorously counter the consensus stemming from this myth, that "doing as the Romans do" when pursuing business abroad is a sign of tolerance – a sign of respect for the other culture. This erroneous and often twisted thinking has unfortunately led to a system of grand, overwhelming, deadly corruption in many parts of the world. Corruption itself is a primary cause of underdevelopment, economic failure and lack of democracy in many parts of the world, in particular in the poorest countries.

Even more astounding: the political class here in Europe and in other rich countries refused and often still refuses to consider as an evil the aiding and abetting of the corruption that they were spreading in the world. On the contrary – they not only condoned corruption, allowed corruption to be legal as long as it was committed outside their own borders, they even allowed it to be tax-deductible and subsidized. Now, fortunately, this situation has changed in many places. The change – a dramatic one – was brought about through a coalition between business, governments and civil society, and has been captured in the form of a convention signed by some thirty members of the OECD and four additional countries, of course, including Germany. So, since early 1999, in a number of these signatory countries which in the meantime have ratified the convention, bribery abroad has become as much of a crime as it is at home.

Has this really changed society? I'm afraid to say that we are racing against time and the closing of a window of opportunity. Many of the actors in the international market are only going along with a moratorium on bribery because they expect that their competitors will also stop bribing. However, we have good reason to doubt that this is happening. So, although the laws in Germany, for example, have been changed and are being implemented, German businessmen, German exporters are complaining that their competitors from other parts of the world are not following the same rules, and that therefore bribery is as essential as ever in the fierce competition to procure a contract. Transparency International has been ranking the 20 foremost exporting countries by their propensity to bribe in order to get contracts.

Now let me state very clearly that there is no culture, no tradition, no value system in the world in which corruption is accepted. Of course, there are traditions of making gifts, of supporting one's friends, one's family, one's extended family, but this has nothing to do with grand corruption as we know it. Grand corruption means that millions of euros, millions of dollars are paid into secret bank accounts for leaders in Africa, in Latin America, in Asia, to get them to make terrible decisions about investment programs, about designing power stations, designing huge infrastructures, ports, pipelines, none of which anybody needs – on the contrary, which are destructive to the ecology in these countries, destructive to the people, destructive to their ability to service their debt. Decisions, in fact, which plunge millions and millions of people into poverty. And this is what we have brought about by going along with the myth that corruption is part of the culture of these societies where we want to do business, and that by encouraging corruption, we are simply respecting the ways of others. A myth which is hypocritical, a myth which is destructive, a myth which is deadly, a myth which is no more than a convenient piece of propaganda which allows many of us to sleep well at night.

We should have zero tolerance for international corruption.

# International Law à la Carte

## Richard Goldstone

Judge, Constitutional Court of South Africa; Former Chief Prosecutor for the UN Tribunals for the former Yugoslavia, The Hague

When the limits of tolerance have been reached, when the global community is no longer prepared to stand back and allow inhuman behaviour, be it Apartheid in South Africa, or 'ethnic cleansing' in Kosovo, what are the rules? Certainly, after the Second World War, it was assumed that the Security Council would be the gatekeeper, and would decide when there should, and when there should not, be military and other forms of intervention. Because of the veto power, this no longer works, and it was for that reason that the NATO powers decided, in respect of Kosovo, to bypass, and thereby very seriously weaken, the United Nations Security Council. There were also moral and political reasons, justifiable reasons, to go behind the charter of the United Nations and intervene. And in a world where this has become necessary, we need to find new rules, to have international rules, so you cannot have one super-power, or ten super-powers, deciding for themselves what the new rules are. What concerns me particularly is that the United States seems to be using international law as some sort of à la carte menu. They invoke whatever items appeal to them, both for others and for themselves; but they ignore whatever items they don't like – and these include the Geneva Conventions. This is exactly what is happening now – an attempt to blackmail the Security Council into granting the United States the right to act outside the law, outside international law and not be judged by the global community. This is a crisis which is devolving very rapidly. The conflict between the U.S. versus other democracies was brought to a head over the International Criminal Court issue, and this is really testing the power of the democratic world to determine whether the United States is going to be able to continue to rule exceptionally, and not apply to itself the rule that it once applied to the rest of the global community.

…Laws regarding intervention are gradually being accepted globally, when human rights violations reach a level that is so severe that the rest of the world is not prepared, and should not be prepared, to sit back and do nothing. And there's a conscience about not having intervened in Rwanda. In fact, I believe it was the non-intervention in Rwanda that made intervention in Kosovo easier. So new norms are being developed. The first concerns the severity of the human rights violations; do they really go beyond tolerance? The second involves exhausting other means, peaceful means, diplomatic means to stop intolerable conduct. The third is making sure that the interveners are not acting for the wrong motives, for selfish motives, but genuinely for humanitarian purposes. The Independent International Commission on Kosovo came to that conclusion in justifying the NATO intervention on political and moral grounds. We examined the relevant thresholds, and they are developing and being discussed more and more.

…My great concern about United States exceptionalism is that it is setting a very bad example to the emerging democracies in the world. It can only be immensely harmful that a democracy, a super-power democracy, is prepared to ignore international rules. For if it does, what is to stop developing countries, developing democracies, from also abandoning international law, which has been, until now, becoming more and more universally accepted?

…My hope for the world lies in democracy. I'm optimistic, because many Americans can openly criticise what is happening in their own country. In non-democracies, this does not happen. Criticism in the United States is not resented, it is accepted, and (as a critic of American policies) I am not regarded as being impertinent, impudent or interfering in the internal affairs of the United States. The same applies in other democracies in Europe. Ultimately, in a democracy, civil society will find its level and will change views. For the last century, the United States has been reticent in joining international organisations, be they world trade organisations or now the International Criminal Court. It took the United States 40 years to ratify the Genocide Convention. However, eventually it comes on board. And it comes on board because the people in a democracy want their country to support the good things that democracies have traditionally stood, and still stand, for. So I believe that the United States will change its mind about the International Criminal Court. It may take a long time, regrettably, but if the ICC works as professionally and efficiently as I'm optimistic it will, the United States will come on board because Americans don't like war criminals, and don't like war crimes being committed.

# America: Flouting Cherished Principles

## Barry Steinhardt
Associate Director, American Civil Liberties Union, New York

I'd like to preface the following comments by saying that I am New Yorker, the offices of the American Civil Liberties Union are about six or seven blocks away from the World Trade Center. I had family members in the building, acquaintances who were killed, so the events of September 11th are very real to me. So too are the issues of security and civil liberties.

I think the United States presents the most dramatic example of the intervention conundrum. Here we have a country which has been variously described either as the last remaining superpower or as a world unto itself, which is now openly flouting many of the principles it claims to champion. These are internationally accepted principles, not only of tolerance, but also of justice and law for its own citizens and for those of other nations, both within and without its borders.

Concrete examples: First, we had the secret round-up of approximately 1200 persons of Middle Eastern or Arab origin. We still don't know the precise number, we still don't know their names, we still don't know what happened to all of them, but we were told that for the most part, they were being held on technical immigration violations. They were kept in secret detention, accorded none of the rights to which they were entitled, either under international law or under American domestic law. None of them had ever been accused of being a terrorist or of being involved in any terrorist activities. Then we had the mass interrogation by federal and local police forces of thousands of non-citizens but legal residents of the United States. To their credit, a number of local police forces refused to co-operate in this mass interrogation, saying, among other things, that not only did it violate the rights of the individuals involved, but it was a foolish police practice because all it would do was alienate the very community that they might want to co-operate with. This mass interrogation of thousands of people produced no evidence of terrorism, no evidence of crime, but it did poison the relationship with a large community in the United States on whom we were counting to assist us in the so-called war on terrorism.

In addition, we have the new guidelines introduced by Attorney General John Ashcroft regarding FBI investigations that permit not only the infiltration but ultimately the disruption of political and religious organisations. These guidelines will be applied most rigorously to mosques in the United States. Then again, we – the United States – are holding hundreds of men in Guantanamo Bay in Cuba. They have not been charged, we refuse to treat them as what they are, namely prisoners of war, we refuse to accord them the rights they are due under the Geneva Convention. We have simply labelled them non-persons, combatants to be left in Guantanamo Bay in Cuba until we are ready to release them, until we declare the war on terrorism to be over – and we have been told that the war on terrorism will never be over. Most recently, we have declared two American citizens – one arrested overseas, one in the United States – to be enemy combatants. We hold them secretly, indefinitely, in defiance of both international and American law.

Finally, I should mention the behaviour of non-government actors. This includes actors such as the four airlines that the American Civil Liberties Union has sued because they removed five persons of Arab or Middle Eastern origin from planes, not because these passengers had failed any security test, not because they posed any real risk, but because one or more of their fellow passengers was offended or made nervous by their presence. All five were simply put on the next plane. We also represent a Muslim woman who was strip-searched at an airport in Illinois, even after she had passed every imaginable security test, because she refused to take off her chador.

That is the present reality of America. So I think the conundrum for the international community is, what can we do about the world's only super-power that flouts not only its own laws, but international laws too? Is there some form of intervention that could in fact be effective? To end on a slightly optimistic note, let me add one brief example of intervention which was perhaps effective to a limited degree. Of the above-mentioned 1200 men who were put into detention in the United States, virtually all of them asked to be deported. The ACLU wrote to a number of embassies, for example, to the Embassy of Pakistan, and urged them to intervene on the behalf of their own citizens. A number of them did, and would have done so even if we had not written to them. Pressure was applied, and it had some effect. Some of the detainees who had been accorded none of the rights to which they were entitled were eventually allowed to leave the country. So I think the international community is going to have to think long and hard about what it does with the world's only super-power when the world's only super-power decides to act on its own and to flout every convention of human rights. It is important that the international community continue to put pressure on the United States to behave in a manner that is consistent with what we say are our principles.

# Without Violence

## Ilija Trojanow
Author, Sofia/Mumbai

I would like to start with a reference to ancient Indian philosophy. There is a concept, central to the Hindu, the Jain and to the Buddhist worlds, which is the concept of ahimsa, usually translated as "being without violence". But actually it means far more than that. It means that naming the other is already violence, defining the stranger as a stranger is violence. If one agrees with that argument, one would come to the conclusion that any kind of identity, which eliminates or excludes other identities is a form of violence. With regard, then, to intervention: I think the question is not whether there should or should not be intervention in any particular case, but rather, what kind of intervention it should be. The way I see it, human history has been the history of increasing interventions, and these interventions have all too often been violent. Western civilisation has a history of bringing genocide to a lot of the world, and that kind of intervention is certainly not the kind of intervention we want to define as a perspective for the future.

What we haven't yet embarked upon, however, is the intervention of humanitarianism. And although we talk about problems that seem insurmountable, I believe that if we were to implement the philosophy of "without violence", many of them might well be quite easy to solve. For example, the question of weapons:

even simple measures such as forbidding the production and distribution of land mines have been vetoed by certain members of the UN. Similarly, the initiative to stop small weapons being sold and distributed. There is so much we could change in the world by intervening in a socially responsible manner, with interventions not dictated by self-interest, egoism and greed. So I believe we should re-define the notion of intervention and come up with effective rules.

…A different question concerns the moral authority of the West to intervene (in the traditional, violent way). Particularly since September 11th, throughout the world there has been great resentment about what is seen as the hypocrisy of the West. I happened to be both in Pakistan and in India in September 2001. It was interesting to note that in both countries, there was considerable popular anger at this perceived hypocrisy of the West. I also happened to be in Rwanda just before the genocide started there. French advisors ran the Rwandan defence ministry. There were French soldiers at the roadblocks and one French officer told me to leave the country because it would soon no longer be safe, and I left just one day before the genocide started. As we later learned, a number of French nationals, among them Mitterrand's son, were heavily involved in selling arms and in co-operating with the Rwandan government at that time. …The trouble is, we are not socially responsible enough to be pro-active and to stand for a policy which would hinder violent developments in the first place. And unless we do that, the people of the world will not feel that the West has the moral authority to intervene.

Wilhelm Heitmeyer, Nigel Barley, Shala Azad,
Peter Frey (moderator), Dr. Motte, Gilles Kepel

# The Path to the Future: Building an Open Mind

*Tolerance, natural or acquired, requires nurturing. Are people born intolerant, with inherent fears of Otherness? Or are they born with unformed but open minds which may be gradually corrupted by their environment?*
*How can we educate people from the start to be tolerant citizens? What can we do to re-educate the millions of young people around the world today who have been raised to hate specific other people and whose very identity is based on intolerance?*

# Building an Open Mind

**Hans Küng**
President, Global Ethic Foundation, Tübingen

I would like to focus on three issues only, on which, I hope, most of you in the audience tend to agree.

**1.** Huntington's much-debated "Clash of Civilizations" delivers a justified warning. It fails, however, to serve as a reliable compass for our future or suggest a new paradigm of international relations. His concept:

· is empirically unproved and untenable; promotes the concept of civilizations as power blocks (the West against Islam or China);

· ignores the overlapping and common aspects of the cultures and religions as well as their interconnections.

**2.** But Huntington is right when he, unlike other sociologists, takes quite seriously the significance of religions to the future of humanity. It is best to view religions in the context of human contradictions: They can act as catalysts in bringing about peace, understanding, and reconciliation (as they did during the upheavals in Eastern Europe, South Africa, Central America). But they can also encourage war, intolerance, and fundamentalism, as they unfortunately have done in ex-Yugoslavia, Northern Ireland, Kashmir and, especially dramatically, in the Middle East, where many political claims are grounded in religion (the borders of Israel, Jerusalem as the capital of Israel). The counterpoint to Huntington's "Clash" would be "The Dialogue of Civilisations and Cultures". There'd be no peace among the nations until there's peace among religions.

**3.** And, finally, the obvious failure of key ideologies that functioned until recently as ersatz religions is particularly important for our future. Imperialism, racism, and nationalism have now no future in those European countries where they have originated.

A new pattern of international relations appears to offer "the path to the future" to the younger generations. I'm not alone in saying this; in fact, my observations only summarise the opinions published in a booklet *Crossing the Divide* which has dealt with the issue of the clash of cultures. The U.N. General Secretary Kofi Annan has asked a 20-member "Group of Eminent Persons" to produce this document for the U.N. General Assembly, and Richard von Weizsäcker and myself have represented Germany and Switzerland in this group. It would be important to note that not a single delegate mentioned the clash of civilizations during the two days of U.N. debate on Nov. 8-9, 2001. Rather, everyone talked about the dialog of civilisations. I believe this new approach aims beyond promoting sheer tolerance. This is why I'm pleased that the conference organisers called this panel "Building an Open Mind."

Their approach has highlighted what by now has become standard: Since 1945, policies of regional understanding, rapprochement and reconciliation have been winning over the policies propelled by nationalism, power and prestige, in which moral norms have played a rather minor role, policies that were launched in Europe by Machiavelli and practiced by such statesmen as Richelieu, Bismarck, Palmerston, Clemenceau and Lloyd George.

France and Germany have implemented the former policies in an exemplary fashion. All the OECD states – from the eastern borders of Germany to Canada to the U.S. and across the globe to New Zealand, Australia and Japan – have been practicing them in such a way that already for more than half a century we have had no war in this vast area.

But the key issue is whether such "peaceful democracy" can

become reality in the world of African, Asian and Islamic cultures. Just imagine: mutual cooperation, willingness to compromise and to integrate will rule in Afghanistan, Kashmir and Middle East instead of confrontation, aggression and revenge that prevail at present.

"Building an Open Mind": This new political arrangement obviously implies a change in mentality that goes well beyond the daily political routine:

Instead of new organisations, a new way of thinking, "a new mindset", "an open mind" is necessary. Indeed, there is a need for a new spiritual approach. National, ethnic and religious diversity should be considered as a potential enrichment, rather than a threat. While the old paradigm was predicated on having an enemy, even an inherited one, the new setup doesn't need an enemy at all. Instead, it implies a partner, a competitor or an opponent. This leads to economic competition on all levels rather than to military confrontation.

It has dawned on many that a nation could reach sustainable prosperity not through war but through peace; not through animosity or indifference but through co-operation.

This realisation has made it possible to implement a policy that will result in a win-win situation rather than in a zero-sum game. Conducting such policy won't be so easy for the younger generation. Politics will remain – however violence-free – "the art of the possible". For it to work, politics has to be based on more than just a "post-modernist", random pluralism that operates according to the principle "anything goes". Rather, it has to be predicated on a social pact encompassing specific basic values, rights and obligations. In order to function, all kinds of social groups have to join such a basic social pact: religious believers and atheists, followers of different faiths, ideologies and philosophies. This pact would have to move far away from the Vatican's rigorous moralising that is fixated on sexuality and preaches rigidly an artificial dogmatic view on everything from birth control to abortion to euthanasia. It would need to contain a minimum of basic ethical imperatives of humanity, without which no social group, however big or small, not even a class of school pupils, can function properly.

A democratic system can't force such a social consensus; on the contrary, it has to be the very basis of it. Moreover, rather than assuming a common ethical system ("ethics"), this consensus indicates the presence of a common ground in basic values and norms, rights and obligations, in other words, the existence of a common ethos ("ethic"), the ethos of mankind. Such a global ethos ("global ethic") doesn't imply a new ideology or some sort of "a superstructure" forced by the West upon "the rest of the world"; no, it is a global ethic that binds together the resources of religions and philosophies from China and India to Europe, binds them not by law but by conscience. Take the Golden Rule, for instance, which found its way into the writings of Confucius 500 years before Christ and into the teachings by Rabbi Hillel 20 years before Christ as well as into the Sermon on the Mount and into the Islamic tradition: "Do unto others, as you would have them do unto you". Such a rule should govern the interaction between states and religions, between social and ethnic groups, not just between individuals.

Such a major learning process should start small. I'm not calling on secondary schools to teach the global ethos; rather, they should practice it as a school ethos in order to improve the general state of morals at schools and thus decrease the pupils' aggressiveness. Fortunately, especially after the Pisa report, there's a lot more awareness in Germany that is is necessary to provide our young generation with moral values and norms that should help keep our society together and protect it from disintegrating. However, the talk of such values as "democracy", "tolerance", and "pluralism" often remains far too vague. Ethos should be as concrete and practical as life itself. True, the roots of violence, greed, and carelessness lie in our society, but they also stem from the mind of man. We have to emphasise certain values and norms that aren't selected at random and are by no means fully culture-specific, especially when the current moment and its conflicts become the issue. Here are, for instance, the four ancient precepts that you can find already in the writings of Patanjali, the founder of Yoga, in the Buddhist canons, as well as in the Judeo-Christian Ten Commandments and in the Koran:

**1.** Because of all the deaths in the territories occupied by Israel and of the deaths in Israel caused by this occupation; because of the shootings in American and European schools, and because of the suicides among Japanese schoolchildren – because of all this, should we not remind everybody of the oldest commandment of all which exists in all the great traditions of humanity: "Thou shalt not kill!" or as a positive admonition "Worship life!"?

**2.** And the corruption that has spread, cancer-like, through business and politics, science and medicine; and the shameless self-serving and insider trading that have reached the top floors of our society – do they not give us sufficient reason to insist urgently that we observe a universal rule: "Thou shalt not steal!" or hark to a positive counsel: "Deal fair and square!"?

**3.** With politicians lying and the mass media manipulating the public, should we not remind everyone about the essential and time-proven religious and philosophical imperative: "Thou shalt not lie!" or, positively expressed: "Speak and act truthfully!"?

**4.** And priests molesting children, and women being sexually exploited – are these not cause enough to emphasise the ancient wisdom that is present in all the ethical and religious teachings:

"Thou shalt not misuse sexuality" or "Respect and love each other!"?

As to the dialogue of civilisations and religions: I have always encouraged and practiced an unconditionally honest dialogue, which doesn't attempt to sweep under the rug such inconvenient topics as:

· how Koran and Sharia treat the issues of violence and war;
· whether the Bible establishes Israel's borders;
· the possibility of salvation outside the fundamentalist Protestant faith or questioning the unicity and salvific universality of Jesus Christ and the Roman-Catholic church, so forcefully reiterated in Vatican's Declaration "Dominus Jesus" (The Lord Jesus)…

Since Vatican II, we in the Christian community have made good progress by engaging the World Church Council in a lively discourse. Under the next Pope, the Catholic Church is hoping to advance further not only in the dialogue between Jews and Christians, but also in the discourse between Christians and Moslems and, hopefully, even between Jews and Moslems. Hopefully! Why do I still have hope?

**1.** Since the barbaric events of September 11th, people everywhere became much more sensitive to a possible misuse of religion. The question "What kind of Islam do you prefer?" is being asked not only in Afghanistan after the formation of its government, but also in many Arab nations, in Europe and in Turkey. As a Sufi creed in Afghanistan, Islam is a moderate religion whose followers have no desire to see Taliban returning to power. And we can assume that the majority of Moslems in other countries also hanker for peace.

**2.** Not only enlightened and reform-orientated adherents of "the cultural Islam" but also conservative religious Moslems are rejecting the concept of conducting a violent holy war ("Djihad") against "the infidels" as well as global Islamisation which aims to spread "Dar al-Islam" ("The House of Islam") throughout the world and turn it thus into "Dar al-Salam" ("The House of Peace"). They are prepared to accept a plurality of religions as long as they themselves can live according to their Islamic tradition.

**3.** We should certainly deal with inequalities between Islamic and Christian ideologies. Those, however, who, like me, belong to a Christian church that until Vatican II acted according to a medieval, counter-reformationist formula that refused to recognise freedom of religion and conscience, should be careful about reproaching Moslems. One could only hope that the Catholic Church and Islam are able to replicate the fundamental shifts in thinking introduced by the Reformation and by modern Enlightenment. If they are successful, non-Moslems in Islamic countries will come to enjoy the same rights and respect as the rest of the population and get rid of their status of a "legally protected" group – which does little but mark their status of second-class citizens and religious worshippers. This is why I agree with Gilles Kepel, who has repeatedly – and loudly – warned of the danger presented by a radical Islamism, while pointing out that it has started declining especially in Iran, Turkey and Algeria – despite recent attempts to re-assert Islam in Nigeria, Ivory Coast and Chechen. Because radical Islamists have shown their inability to take power, their popularity among the population in those countries has suffered. At the same time, we can hope that the efforts to reconcile Islam with democracy ("an Islamic democracy" could be rather similar to "a Christian democracy") will bear fruit. Thomas L. Friedman shared this view when he wrote about Iran in the June 19th issue of the *New York Times*: "You find democratic reformers who have learned from the shah's failed attempt at imposed secularism, and from the past 23 years of Islamic rule, that no democracy will take root in Iran that doesn't find a respected place for Islam. And you find religious thinkers who have also learned from the last 23 years that Iranians have lived through enough incompetent clerics trying to run a government – and trying to tell people what they should wear, think and speak – to know that Islam can't regulate every aspect of a nation's life in the modern age without producing a backlash."

I'd like to end with two short quotes from *Crossing the Divide*, the manifesto we wrote for the United Nations:
"If we have failed to overcome that which divides us and to realise that 'different' does not mean 'adversary', then we have built new walls rather than destroyed old ones. This doesn't necessarily mean that new generations shouldn't try turning the walls into bridges and use them to cross the divide. The least a future generation can do is to deal with the issues the previous generation has failed completely or partially to cope with. But the younger generation will see as arrogant those who are making fun of our efforts to bridge the gap caused by 'us' and 'them', by 'friend' and 'enemy', to move beyond such basic human concepts. An example of such arrogance is the opinion that what has been achieved represents the best of all possible worlds… Whether we happen to justify the clash of cultures or to rise united against those who kill innocent people only because they are different, is strictly up to each of us… Our children could fare better than us. They could get where we haven't been, they could achieve what we have failed to, and they could discover what we've never even thought has existed. They could give human solidarity a new form and raise the common human denominator. Many of them will bridge gaps, until one day there will be many, many bridges and no more walls.

The vision we are offering is not an announcement, a declaration, or a plea – it is a well-grounded argument. Rather, it is an ethically-orientated vision of life that has been developing step by step. We are already moving in this direction."

# Change in Afghanistan: a Long Process

Representative of RAWA (Revolutionary Association of the Women of Afghanistan), Quetta

The people of Afghanistan suffered enormously over the past twenty-five years, first during the Soviet occupation, then during the fundamentalist government in Afghanistan from 1992 and under the Taliban, too. But throughout all of these years the international community remained completely silent towards the situation in the country. When finally it started taking an interest, it dismissed many of our problems by saying that it was part of the cultural tradition of the country to kill each other and to fight against each other, because there are so many different, warring ethnic groups. It was only after September 11th that the world realised the danger of fundamentalism and terrorism in Afghanistan and started taking action against it.

In the meantime, in the past year, there have been some changes in the country, but they have been very small indeed. The problems we had were not just the ones you hear about on television: the boycott on music or the like. The biggest problem still remains: the existence of fundamentalism – the fundamentalism that yesterday went under the name Taliban and today under the name of the Northern Alliance. These fundamentalists still have the military and political power today. If there have been some small changes, they are only in Kabul, which is under the control of international forces. It is of course true that education is the most important weapon in our hands. It is the most important tool we have to change society, to achieve freedom, democracy and prosperity. But the Afghan nation, mentally and physically, has been destroyed in the last twenty-five years. It will take a long time, with a lot of sacrifices, to repair some of the damage and change the way the people feel and think.

What we desperately need in Afghanistan are universal values such as women's rights, human rights, democracy and freedom. No one can say that these are Western values or Eastern values, they are human values. Once these values have been introduced, even though we are a backward culture and our men have closed minds, we will succeed in changing the nation. Through education and increased awareness, it will be possible to change the dreams and the hopes of the younger generation. However, this will not happen overnight. For twenty-five years, most young boys aged nine, ten and eleven were sent to the different fronts to join the different military groups. And they were raised not like educated citizens, but like criminals and warlords. And today they have the power, and they can do whatever they want with their guns. This is our reality.

…I did not go to university, but I went to school in Pakistan. My education was very different from that of girls in Afghanistan. And because I had a good education, I can be a voice for my people wherever I go.

# The Pull of the Mall

## Nigel Barley

Author; Assistant Keeper, Ethnology Department, British Museum, London

I am a firm believer that the apparently ephemeral, the apparently passing, the apparently unimportant, can actually be decisive in deciding the courses of our lives. It was not the clash of ideologies that brought the Berlin Wall down, it was not different points of view. It was actually shopping. And it was the urge to go shopping, the simple delight that people take in going out and enjoying themselves, the pleasures of the shopping mall – the cutting edge of globalisation – that did more to destroy the Wall than all the serious debates. And I firmly believe that one day we will be saved from the evils of war, not by international accords but simply because chartered accountants will prove to us that we can simply no longer afford it.

... It is interesting that international bodies, international conferences tend to make very general and very bland statements that everyone can agree to. If you say "thou shalt not kill", most people will agree to that, yet people kill all over the world. It is the circumstances in which killing is permitted that they do not agree about. When you are defending yourself, when you are defending someone else, when you put on the uniform of your nation's army, when a judge tells you to, you are allowed to kill. So it is not really the big statements that are controversial, it is the way they are encountered, the way the principles are put into everyday life. An example: There is a school in the north of England where there is a high percentage of Muslim immigrants and, therefore, Muslim children. And, of course, those Muslim children can eat only Halal food. There was much discussion about what to do about this. And the Christian governors of the school decided that it was no problem for Christian children to eat Halal food, so let everybody eat Halal food. The problem was solved. It was a triumph for tolerance. Then one of the governors went to see how the animals were killed to make the food Halal and decided that it was completely cruel and unnatural and therefore could not be countenanced. So in the interest of the rights of the animals, the rights of the children came into question. Now that seems absurd, but in the real world that is exactly what happens. In the real world, principles and values frequently conflict and frequently undermine each other. So I don't think we are ever going to solve the problem of intolerance. Nor do I think we should be too tough on ourselves if we fail to solve it. It's as my doctor says to me: "You know, you come here, you tell me you feel terrible, I feel terrible, everybody feels terrible, it's a sign that your health is perfectly normal."

… There is a horrible tokenism in the air about respect. An illustration: In a letter sent back to London by an 18th century English governor of the British colony in Indonesia, he said: "I have no problem with local rulers. I treat them in every way as any sensible man treats his wife. In matters of no importance, I am full of consideration and show them great respect. In matters that have the slightest financial implications, I remain totally inflexible." A wonderful example of crass prejudice.

I really do believe that at certain points, different views of the world impinge on each other, and it's not enough to dance around them and pour the sauce of tolerance over them. They do have to be talked about. They do have to be confronted. And a modus vivendi has to be found. That is not easy. Both tolerance and intolerance have their emotional and their logical components. No one is more logical than a fanatic, an intolerant fanatic

...I am absolutely staggered at the way that English football supporters – I don't want to say hooligans – were totally overwhelmed by the sheer orderliness and niceness of public life in Japan, and found themselves forced to behave in a nice way. But a warning: We should not forget that during the First World War, at Christmas, all the troops came out from the different armies and played football in no man's land, and the generals were terrified. They thought, this is the end of the war, these men are not going to obey us any longer. But fortunately for the generals, when Christmas was over, the troops quietly went back to their lines and started killing each other again.

# The Risks of Tolerance

## Wilhelm Heitmeyer
Director, Institute for Interdisciplinary Research on Conflict and Violence, Bielefeld

Tolerance often emphasises cultural differences and reinforces social inequalities. The idea of tolerance always includes the differences of power between majority and minority. The majority can obviously tolerate the minority, but from the opposite perspective it is obviously absurd to think that a minority can tolerate a majority.

This means that tolerance is a unilateral process. On the other hand, establishing relationships based on mutual recognition is a relatively laborious multilateral process which is carried out by means of regulating conflict. However, our society is obviously not at the moment ready to engage actively in such a process. Instead, we make gestures of tolerance, which are to some extent hypocritical and give rise to understandable anger among the immigrants. Therefore we must seriously address the question: how do we organise relationships and processes based on mutual recognition?

To do this, controlled conflicts are necessary, since modern society is held together not by mutual values nor by a prevailing culture, but by controlled conflicts, which everyone endures together. It is only in this way that the opposing parties can each become conscious of their own positions. However, it is precisely this situation that is often concealed by a veil of 'tolerance'. But we must face up to the conflict – and we must remember that we need not always regard conflict as being destructive. A controlled conflict requires three conditions: firstly, a background of consensus; secondly, institutions that can conduct this conflict long-term and in a meaningful way; and thirdly 'cross cuttings', that is people who transcend the borders between the different cultures and origins. The concept of the equal value and the integrity of the individual person must be an integral element of controlled conflict.

# The Rule of Respect

## Dr. Motte

DJ and Founder of the Love Parade, Berlin

At the Berlin Love Parade, which has taken place every year since 1989 and is becoming more and more international, everyone moves around freely. People can do what they like. The Love Parade only has one rule: Respect. And so the Love Parade lives out something which society at large ought also to put into practice. We don't just look for the things that divide us or make us different, but keep our eyes firmly fixed on what we have in common.

With our music we have created a social space for ourselves on the streets. We play an important cultural role in Germany. And our message is understood in other places, too. When I talk to young people abroad, I discover that when they think of Germany, the first thing that comes to mind is the young people who share their joie de vivre in the Love Parade, who bring their own music with them on their floats, and simply use the parade to have fun. In the meantime, Love Parades have been held in Mexico City, Vienna, Cape town and Tel Aviv. And if the people of Kabul want it, there will soon be a Love Parade in Kabul, too.

# Hope for the European Model

## Gilles Kepel
Professor, Institut d'Etudes Politiques, Paris

There was not all that much violence in France after September 11th. Certainly, there was violence against some Jewish places of worship. But I do not think this should be seen as the failure of integration, the failure of the French model. It was something that was deeply related to what was happening in the Middle East at the time. It was caused primarily by young kids from North Africa who sat watching television all day and thinking they should do something to show their brothers in Palestine some sort of solidarity. This violence was regrettable and had to be dealt with by the police. But we should not exaggerate and conclude, as did the American press at the time, that France, and Europe in general, were becoming beacons of anti-Semitism.

… (It is true that) young kids from North Africa identified more with what they saw on television than with their immediate, local surroundings. In the past, North African Moslems and Jews lived together in the outskirts of a number of large French cities and there was a level of accommodation and a level of friction. And then the events in the Middle East ignited tensions between the two groups.

(On his theory that the Islamic movement has passed its peak because of its propensity towards violence) Given what they set out to achieve, Islamic (fundamentalist) movements since September 11th do not have an impressive record. The Taliban regime has been wiped out. The Muslim world did not come together to demonstrate solidarity with Afghanistan against the West. And even in Palestine, when militants want to turn the second Intifada into a general jihad against the Israelis with their suicide attacks, they have not succeeded. The results for the Palestinians are disastrous, and their ability to negotiate with the Israelis has never been so low. I think we have to think of terrorism or the use of terrorism in political terms. When the Rote Armee Fraktion used terrorism, it was because they had a goal, they wanted to build up a constituency, to show the exploited masses of Germany, who had gone to sleep under Social Democrats, that they had to wake up and fight against the bourgeoisie. So they used terror, and it was very violent and shocking at the time. But at the end of the day, they did not manage to develop a political movement. And this is the same situation we have today in the Muslim world.

After the so-called success in Afghanistan that ended in 1989 with the pullout of the Soviet troops, there came a series of failures of the various jihads – in Algeria, in Bosnia, in Egypt, in the first half of the 1990s. And after that, the militant groups used terror to build up a local constituency, to try to take over their countries. But they have not been successful. They have managed to spread havoc in the West – but that has been a temporary victory, I think. It says nothing about the increasing strength of Islamic movements worldwide.

(On active tolerance) What is striking about the Muslim population in France is the incredible amount of intermarriage. Whereas Pakistanis marry Pakistanis in Britain, and Turks marry Turks in Germany, a great many young girls and boys of North African origin cohabit with, or marry, partners of true French stock. This is not a tolerance issue, it is just an issue of living together and building a society together.

(On inner values) I think that the values of the Europe of today and the Europe of tomorrow are but a blend of the values which were inherited by all of us who came to Europe, and which we are continuing to build on in our interaction. Any page of the Paris telephone book shows clearly just how many of us do not come from French stock. And we are building the fabric of France, the fabric of Europe today and tomorrow. Clearly, this building together is accompanied by a certain amount of conflict. However, I am rather optimistic that because our European model produces comfort, because it produces riches, growth and wealth, it will ultimately win. And, in spite of the all the setbacks (the acts of violence and terror which of course we have to deal with), I don't think we have to be frightened by the challenges. We don't have to submit to everything in the name of multiculturalism. We have to accommodate to the point that we are able to build a shared culture of tomorrow.

# Armin Nassehi

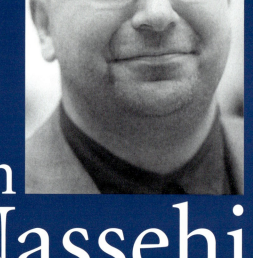

Chairman, Department of Sociology,
Ludwig-Maximilians-University, Munich

# | The Paradox of Tolerance

In my opinion, tolerance and diversity cannot be mandated. They cannot be force-implemented. Tolerance is not a normative concept, it is primarily a symptom, a result, of specific social circumstances in which people do not experience diversity or unexpected events as a threat. I feel that everyday life in modern societies is often more simple than our intellectual and elitist prejudices of reflexive identities and self-analysing life forms allow us to imagine. Real life takes place in neighbourhoods, in small spaces. It is a day-by-day practice. And that tolerance is intimately related to social inequality and satisfaction with ones own life can hardly be called into question. It is important to keep in mind that this is not a question of an objective level of welfare and prosperity, but of the subjective expectations of future stability in a world that seems to have abolished stability, and that is changing faster than the generations. Probably the only adequate measure for a tolerant society is the degree of social mobility and class diffusion that is not conditional on ethnic descent. And this all applies to immigrants as well. It is an intellectual prejudice to think of migrants as a kind of epistemological elite of people with a broader view of life. Often they are quite the opposite.

There is a strange paradox of tolerance. The postulate for tolerance for something or someone is often combined with a strange kind of arrogance. You have to tolerate only what you cannot really accept, or what you experience as being out of order. The paradoxical effect of strategies of tolerance can often result in the very opposite of what they aim to create. The tolerated side can feel tolerance as a subtle form of inequality. For example, tell a member of an ethnic minority that you tolerate him or her as a citizen. Or tell a black man or woman that you tolerate him or her as a complete human being. Or tell a disabled person that you tolerate disabilities. This kind of tolerance is the attitude of a majority towards a minority. The paradoxical effect is that we cannot avoid this strange asymmetry. We have only to mention the neurotic behaviour most Germans show if they talk about, or with, people who are Jewish. In other words, the best-intended efforts unavoidably get caught in this paradox. We therefore have to be aware of the paradox-trap. We in the West are best equipped to observe, and be sensitive to, just how asymmetrically structured the political and often intellectual debates about globalisation, world society and global commitment are.

Diversity, the second key concept, leads us to similar problems. Whenever we hear diversity and it is not in the context of gender, we automatically hear ethnic, or national or even racial diversity. Why don't we, both in business and public affairs, also talk about interdisciplinary diversity, age diversity, intellectual diversity? The discourse of ethnic and national diversity paradoxically increases ethnic and national differences. This discourse plays up what it wants to play down. This discourse is, whether we so desire it or not, part of that standardising discourse of cultural uniqueness. It is part of what we can call identity politics. This is the real challenge for any discussion about tolerance and diversity. I believe that those of us from the West (and I count myself as a Westerner despite my partly non-Western origins) have a responsibility to face our own past – our colonial past, our past of wars and genocide and imperialistic strategies – to get a better feeling for how our own liberal, rational, individualistic and self-controlled self-understanding has historically developed.

The reality of immigration in Germany provides evidence of considerable contradictions. Until very recently the Federal Republic still quite obstinately refused even to recognise the reality of its immigration. But now the realisation that immigrants are simply there is beginning to dawn, and that they are there not just as something that could be hived off under headings like varia et curiosa. By now immigrants have instead become an autochthonous element in our country. Germany – even if this emotive phrase gives rise to anxiety – has been a country of immigration for a long time. A reality that has become stable over a period of forty years cannot simply be ignored. About half of these more than 7 million foreigners have been living in Germany for more than 10 years, and about a third of them longer than 20 years. These facts do seem to give rise to a certain amount of surprise among the political public.

The drama of immigration usually tells a story full of problems and unpleasantness. Something that represents the selling out of the home country and the danger of being swamped by foreigners to some people is for others a cause of serious concern and reservations. As a result, immigration does not get a very good press from either side. Certainly the fact that immigration into the Federal republic has remained politically unnoticed for so long also shows how well-developed the flexibility and adaptability of modern society is, even if there was no political intention at all to be so. There can be no doubt that many immigrants live in very precarious circumstances. At the same time, a considerable gap is beginning to open within the immigrant group. A large proportion of the original immigrants and their descendants have settled in the Federal Republic and lead – just like the native population – both fortunate and disastrous lives. Second and third generation immigrants can be found both as entrepreneurs and as students at university, they can be found as authors writing in the German language (sic!), as well as young people speaking with Bavarian, Swabian, Westphalian or Berlin accents. The institutions of the welfare state, the law, the economy, religion and not least education have exerted a strong inclusive pressure, which has not permitted complete segregation of the immigrant population in spite of their political marginalisation. Many immigrants in major conurbations do in fact still live in concentrated and segregated areas. The diffusion of immigrants and their descendants within the education system is absolutely catastrophic, but this has more to do with the education system in Germany itself, which in international terms is very stratified, than with the immigrant background of the young people affected by it.

In spite of all its home-grown problems, Germany as a 'country of non-immigration' can in no way be compared with the ways ghettoisation takes place in countries that have declared themselves to be countries of immigration. Moreover, the immigrants' own segregation and strong group-formation should not always be interpreted simply in the sense of isolation from 'German' society – given that the native population also does not live in 'German' spaces, but in social spaces that correspond to their respective milieus, similarities and achievable opportunities. If the 'bourgeois privilege of otherness' is one of the constitutive experiences of modern life-situations, then immigrants can at times only move truly invisibly among their peers, thus claiming precisely this bourgeois privilege.

Elsewhere immigrants are visible – and the well-meant call for 'Tolerance' makes them even more visible. This specifically German example shows that there is one thing that immigrants and their descendants do not need in Germany, and that is tolerance. They have a far greater need for the kind of recognition of a legal, political and economic nature that befits a modern society.

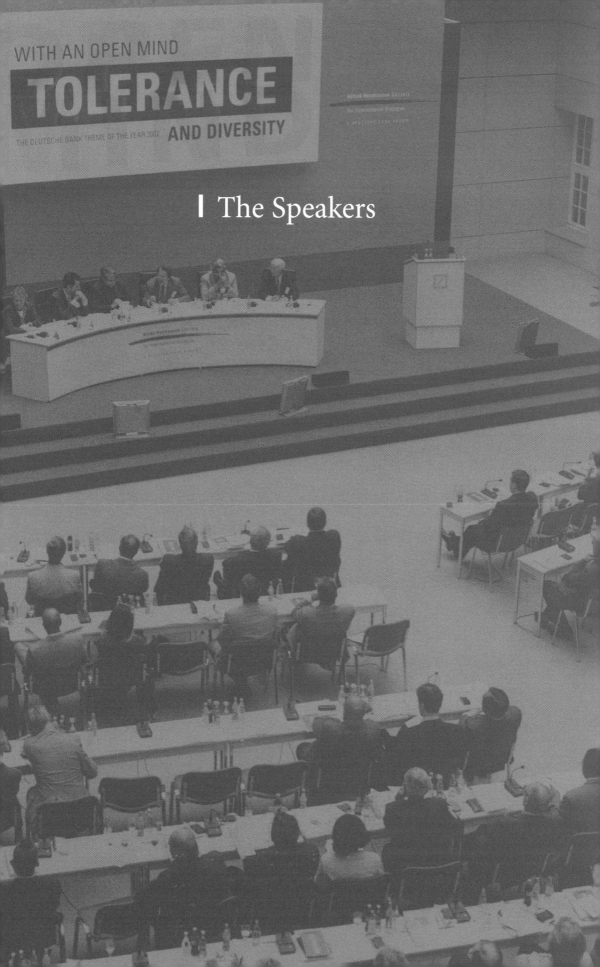

# I The Speakers

## THE SPEAKERS

### Jeffrey Abramson
Louis Stulberg Professor of Law and Politics, Brandeis University, Boston

Born in 1947 in Philadelphia. Ph.D. in political theory, J. D., Harvard. Clerked for the Chief Justice of the California Supreme Court and served as Special Assistant to the Attorney General, Massachusetts. Frequent contributor to the op-ed page of the *New York Times*. Selected publications: *Liberation and its Limits: The Moral and Political Thought of Freud*; *The Electronic Commonwealth: The Impact of New Media Technologies on Democratic Values*; *We, the Jury: The Jury System and the Ideal of Democracy*.

### Josef Ackermann
Spokesman of the Board of Managing Directors, Deutsche Bank, Frankfurt

Born 1948 in Mels/Switzerland. Since 1996, Member of the Board of Managing Directors. Since 2002, Spokesman of the Board of Managing Directors and of the Group Executive Committee of Deutsche Bank; Chairman of the Board of Trustees of the Alfred Herrhausen Society for International Dialogue.

### Tariq Ali
Author, London

Born 1943 in Lahore. Studied politics and philosophy in Pakistan and Oxford. Because of his committed opposition to the military dictatorship in Pakistan, was forced into exile in England. As a member of the Bertrand Russell Foundation for Peace, was one of the initiators of the solidarity campaign for Vietnam. Intellectual force behind the international student movement. Author of historical, political and biographical books focussing on international history and Islam, recently *The Clash of Fundamentalisms*. Also writes novels, screenplays and theatrical plays.

### Shala Azad (fictitious name)
Representative of RAWA (Revolutionary Association of the Women of Afghanistan), Quetta

Born in 1974 in Kabul, Afghanistan. A member of the cultural committee of RAWA, she is involved in publishing as well as in event and demonstration planning. Educated in Pakistan, she now teaches in a refugee camp school. She is dedicated to enlightening Afghan women. She represents RAWA at events throughout the world.

### Benjamin R. Barber
Kekst Professor of Civil Society, University of Maryland,
and Principal, Democracy Collaborative, New York

Gershon and Carrol Kekst Professor of Civil Society at the University of Maryland and one of the directors of the Democracy Collaborative with offices in New York, Washington and at the University of Maryland. Devotes himself to the basic issues of democratic society. His publications include *Strong Democracy: Participatory Politics for a New Age* and *Jihad vs. McWorld*, in which he analyses the processes of globalisation. In the spring of 2002 DaimlerChrysler Fellow at the American Academy.

## THE SPEAKERS

### Nigel Barley
Author; Assistant Keeper, Ethnology Department, British Museum, London

Born in 1947 in the United Kingdom. Studied modern languages at Trinity College, Cambridge. 1975-1977 lecturer in anthropology at University College London. Joined the British Museum in 1980. Fieldwork research in Cameroon, Nigeria, Ghana, Indonesia, Malaysia. Writer and broadcaster. Author of *The Innocent Anthropologist*, *The Duke of Puddle Dock* and *White Rajah*.

### Soheib Bencheikh
Grand Mufti, Marseilles

Born 1961 in Jeddah, Saudi Arabia. Studied at universities in Cairo (Al-Azhar), Brussels and at the Sorbonne in Paris. Received doctorate in religious studies from the Sorbonne. Appointed Grand Mufti of Marseilles in 1999 by the Director of the Paris Mosque, Dalil Boubakeur. Calls for a radical reform of Islam to bring about the reconciliation of Islam with Modernity. Author of *Marianne et le Prophète*.

### Rama Bijapurkar
Founder and Chairperson, Management Consulting, Mumbai

Born in 1957 in Hyderabad, India. Worked with McKinsey and Company and MARG, India's largest market research company. Has published extensively on marketing strategy and consumer research issues in international market research forums and is frequently quoted in international publications. Set up her own strategy consulting practice and is a director on the board of four of India's leading corporates. Serves on the board of Give Foundation, a non-profit organisation, and is a visiting professor at the Indian Institute of Management, Ahmedabad.

### Roger van Boxtel
Minister for Urban Policy and Integration of Ethnic Minorities, The Hague

Born in 1954 in Tilburg, Holland. Studied medicine and law at the University of Amsterdam. 1981-1986 worked for the Union of Dutch Local Authorities (VNG). 1986-1994 management consultant with Verlinden Wezeman, Ernst & Whitney and Anderson Ellfers Felix. Various positions within his party, Democrats 66 (D66). Since 1994 member of the lower house of parliament. Has been involved in non-profit bodies such as the POA and the "Tot en Met" organisation. From 1998 to 2002, Minister for Urban Policy and Integration of Ethnic Minorities in the Dutch government.

# THE SPEAKERS

### Fyodor Burlatsky
Chairman, Scientific Council for Political Studies, Moscow

Born in 1927 in Kiev, Ukraine. Ph.D., professor since 1967. 1960-1964 speechwriter and adviser on foreign affairs for Nikita Khrushchev. 1982-1991 political observer and editor-in-chief, *Literaturnaia Gazeta*. 1987-1993 chairman of the DeBurg International Commission on Human Rights. Since 1995 chairman of the Scientific Council for Political Science of the Presidium of the Russian Academy of Sciences. Professor at Heidelberg University, Cambridge University, St. Antony's College, Oxford University, etc. Author of numerous books.

### Ian Buruma
Journalist and Author, London

Born in 1951 in The Hague, Holland. Educated in Holland and Japan, spent many years living and travelling in Asia. Long-time observer of cultural and ethnic issues in East and West. Writes extensively for *The New York Review of Books* and *The Guardian*. Selected publications: *God's Dust: A Modern Asian Journey; A Japanese Mirror: Heroes and Villains of Japanese Culture; The Wages of Guilt: Memories of War in Germany and Japan; The Missionary and the Libertine; Bad Elements: Chinese Rebels from Los Angeles to Beijing*.

### Daniel Cohn-Bendit
MEP, Les Verts, Strasbourg/Brussels

Born in 1945 in Montauban, France. Studied sociology at the University of Nanterre. 1968 leader of the May Revolution in Paris, deported from France. 1968-1973 bookseller in Frankfurt/Main. 1976 editor and publisher of the magazine *Pflasterstrand*. 1989-1996 honorary head of department in the Office for Multicultural Affairs. Since 1994 presenter of the Swiss television programme "Literaturclub". 1994-1999 Member of the European Parliament for Bündnis 90/Die Grünen. Since 1999 Member of the European Parliament for Les Verts, since 2002 co-chairman of the parliamentary group.

### Dan Diner
Professor of History, The Hebrew University of Jerusalem, and Director, Simon Dubnow Institute, University of Leipzig

Born in 1946. Awarded doctorate in 1973, habilitation in 1980. Professor at the University of Odense, Denmark; University of Essen 1985-1999; University of Tel Aviv 1988-2000, where he was director of the Institute for German History 1994-2000. Since 1999 director of the Simon Dubnow Institute for Jewish History and Culture at the University of Leipzig and professor at the history department there. Author and editor of numerous publications on 20th century German and European history, on Jewish history and on the history of the Middle East.

# THE SPEAKERS

### Assia Djebar
Author; Lecturer, Department of French, New York University

Born in 1936 in Algeria. The first Algerian woman to be admitted into the exclusive Ecole Normale Supérieure in Paris. Lecturer in French Studies at New York University. Currently rated as the top female writer in the Maghreb. Recipient of numerous prizes, most recently the Peace Prize of the Association of the German Book Trade in 2000. Seeks to retrace in her narratives the fight for liberation led by women of her native Algeria. Selected publications: *Women of Algiers in Their Apartment, Fantasia* and *Algerian White*.

### Peter Eigen
Founder and Chairman of the Board, Transparency International, Berlin

Born in 1938 in Augsburg. Studied law, economics and political science, doctorate from Frankfurt. Worked in economic development at the World Bank. Founder of TI, a global NGO fighting against corruption, with over 80 national chapters worldwide. Research and teaching at Frankfurt University, Harvard, Johns Hopkins and Free University Berlin. Honorary doctorate from the Open University (UK). Member of advisory groups: CID, Harvard University; World Movement for Democracy; World Trade Organisation. Numerous publications on global governance, specially on corruption.

### Peter Frey
Head of the ZDF Studio, Berlin

Born in 1957. Studied in Mainz and Madrid. 1978-1983 reporter and anchorman at Südwestfunk as well as editor and reporter at Frankfurter Rundschau. Since 1983, reporter and editor of the ZDF news show "Heute-Journal". 1991-1992 deputy director of the ZDF studio in Washington, D.C. Head and anchor of the ZDF national TV news show "Morgenmagazin". 1998-2001 head of the ZDF foreign policy desk and anchor of "Auslandsjournal". Since 2001, head of the Berlin ZDF studio. Author of *From Baghdad to St. Petersburg. My Travel Diary*.

### Peter C. Goldmark
Chairman and CEO, International Herald Tribune, Paris

Born in 1940 in New York. Graduated in government studies from Harvard College in 1962. For four years Secretary of Human Services for the Commonwealth of Massachusetts. 1975-1977 Director of the Budget for the State of New York. 1977-1985 Executive Director of The Port Authority of New York and New Jersey. 1985 joined Times Mirror Company and became Senior Vice President for Eastern Newspapers. 1988-1997 President of The Rockefeller Foundation. Since 1998 Chairman and Chief Executive Officer of the *International Herald Tribune*.

## THE SPEAKERS

### Richard J. Goldstone
Judge, Constitutional Court of South Africa; Former Chief Prosecutor for the UN Tribunals for the former Yugoslavia, The Hague

Born in 1938 in South Africa. Graduated in 1962 from the University of the Witwatersrand. 1991-1994 chaired the Commission of Inquiry regarding Public Violence and Intimidation (Goldstone Comission). 1994-1996 Chief Prosecutor of the UN International Criminal Tribunals for the former Yugoslavia and Rwanda. 1999-2001 chaired the International Independent Inquiry on Kosovo. Since 2001 chairperson of the Task Force on International Terrorism established by the International Bar Association. Recipient of many awards, including the International Human Rights Award of the American Bar Association. Heads the board of the Human Rights Institute of South Africa.

### Stephen E. Hanson
Associate Professor, Department of Political Science, University of Washington, Seattle

Born in 1963. Ph.D. from the University of California, Berkeley. Associate Professor in the Department of Political Science and Director of the Russian, East European and Central Asian Studies (REECAS) Program of the Jackson School of International Studies at the University of Washington. Author of *Time and Revolution: Marxism and the Design of Soviet Institutions,* which received the Wayne S. Vucinich book award from the American Association for the Advancement of Slavic Studies in 1998. Many publications analysing post-communist Russia.

### Wilhelm Heitmeyer
Director, Institute for Interdisciplinary Research on Conflict and Violence, Bielefeld

Born in 1945. Professor of Sociology at the University of Bielefeld and head of its Institute for Interdisciplinary Research on Conflict and Violence. His research concentrates on right-wing extremism, ethno-cultural conflicts, xenophobia and violence. Managing publisher of the publication series *Jugendforschung* and *Kultur und Konflikt.* Author of several books, including *Was hält die Gesellschaft zusammen? – Was treibt die Gesellschaft auseinander?.*

### Tessen von Heydebreck
Member of the Board of Managing Directors, Deutsche Bank, Frankfurt

Born in 1945 in Orth, Pomerania. Studied law in Freiburg and Göttingen, 1975 doctorate in Göttingen. Worked in management for various main branches of the Deutsche Bank, since 1995 member of the Executive Board. Since 2002 also member of the Group Executive Committee, as Chief Administrative Officer responsible for legal affairs, compliance and revision, also Chief Human Resources Officer. Posts at BASF AG, Dürr AG, Gruner+Jahr AG and Nestlé Deutschland AG.

THE SPEAKERS

### Gilles Kepel
Professor, Institut d'Etudes Politiques, Paris

Born 1955 in Paris. Studied Arabic, English and philosophy at the Institut d'Etudes Poltiques de Paris (IEP), doctorate in sociology and political science. Professor at the IEP, Head of the Postgraduate Programmes for Arabic and Muslim Studies and Head of Research at CERI/CNRS. International reputation as expert in Islamic fundamentalism. Several visiting professorships at New York University, Columbia University and others. Numerous publications, recently *Djihad: The Trail of Political Islam*.

### Imre Kertész
Author; Winner of the Nobel Prize for Literature 2002, Budapest

Born in 1929 in Budapest. Deported to Auschwitz 1944, freed from Buchenwald in 1945. From 1948 worked as a journalist, since 1953 as a free-lance writer. In 1975 *Fateless* appeared, which was officially hushed up in Hungary but read intensively in underground literary circles. In 1990 *Kaddish for a Child Not Born* was published in Hungary. Received numerous awards for his work, among them the Leipzig Book Award for European Understanding in 1997.

### Hans Küng
President, Global Ethic Foundation, Tübingen

Born in 1928 in Sursee, Switzerland. Studied philosophy and theology in Rome and Paris. 1960-1996 Professor of Fundamental Theology and Ecumenical Theology at the University of Tübingen. Visiting Professor at universities in New York, Basel, Chicago, Ann Arbor, and Houston. Since 1995 President of the Global Ethic Foundation. Author of numerous books, including *Projekt Weltethos, Weltethos für Weltpolitik und Weltwirtschaft*. Recipient of many awards and honorary doctorates.

### Daniel Libeskind
Architect, Berlin

Born in 1946 in Poland. U.S. citizen since 1965. Studied music and architecture. Graduated in 1970 with a degree in architecture from the Cooper Union College in New York and in 1972 with a postgraduate degree in history and theory of architecture at the School of Comparative Studies at Essex University. His practice extends from building major cultural institutions including museums and concert halls, landscape and urban projects, to stage design, installations and exhibitions. He is the architect of the much-acclaimed Jewish Museum Berlin, the Felix-Nussbaum-Haus, Osnabrück, and the Imperial War Museum North, Manchester.

THE SPEAKERS

### Harriet Mandel

Director, Israel and International Affairs, Jewish Community Relations Council, New York

Born in 1943 in New York. Earned B.A. in Arabic and Islamic studies, M.A. in International and Public Affairs, and an advanced certificate from the Middle East Institute at Columbia University, New York. Since 1986 Director of Israel and International Affairs at Jewish Community Relations Council of N.Y. Member of several Middle East task forces, foreign policy consultant. Participant in public and background meetings with U.S. government officials and high-ranking diplomats in the U.S. and abroad.

### Paul S. Miller

Commissioner, U.S. Equal Employment Opportunity Commission, Washington D.C.

Born in 1961. Graduated in English and history from the University of Pennsylvania and received his law degree from Harvard Law School. Litigator for a Los Angeles law firm, then Director of Litigation for the Western Law Center for Disability Rights. Law professor at Loyola Law School and at the University of California, Los Angeles. Served in President Clinton's White House. Since 1994 Commissioner of the U.S. Equal Employment Opportunity Commission. Has written many scholarly articles on discrimination and civil rights issues.

© Tina Winkhaus-Kuhn

### Dr. Motte

DJ and Founder of the Love Parade, Berlin

Born Matthias Roeingh in 1960 in Berlin. Since 1985 active as DJ. In 1989 founded and organised the first Love Parade in Berlin. In the following years, produced several successful hits. In 1997 awarded the Viva Comet Award at the music fair PopKomm in Cologne. In 1998 produced his first video clip and his first radio show "Love Parade Countdown". In 1999 awarded the BZ-Culture Prize and the Bambi. 2001 founded the "Praxxiz" label. Initiator of several charity events and exhibitions.

### Armin Nassehi

Chairman, Department of Sociology, Ludwig-Maximilians-University, Munich

Born in 1960 in Tübingen. First studied education, received his doctorate in philosophy and is now professor of sociology at the Ludwig- Maximilians-University, Munich. Fields of concentration: Sociological Theory, Social Theory, Migration Sociology, Biography Research, Sociological Thanatology. Author of a number of books, including *Nation, Ethnie, Minderheit. Diskussionen zur Aktualität ethnischer Konflikte*.

## THE SPEAKERS

### Vural Öger
Founder and Director, Öger Tours, Hamburg

Born in 1942 in Ankara. Studied at the Faculty of Mining and Metallurgy at the TU Berlin. 1968 completed his studies and graduated as Diplom-Ingenieur. 1969 founded a Hamburg-based travel agency specialised in tourism to Turkey. 1982 founded Öger Tours GmbH, now Europe's top specialist for Turkey. Since 2000 member of the Federal Government's New Immigrants Commission. In 2001, awarded the Order of Merit of the Federal Republic of Germany by Federal President Johannes Rau for his outstanding services to integration and understanding between different cultures.

### Kenichi Ohmae
Chancellor's Professor of Public Policy, School of Public and Social Research, University of California, Los Angeles

Long-standing president of McKinsey & Company in Tokyo. Works today as international corporate strategist and adviser to the Japanese government. In 1992 founded the reform movement "Heisei Ishin no kai", which strongly advocates radical political reforms. Regularly publishes reform proposals and analyses in the *Wall Street Journal, the New York Times and Newsweek.* Author of numerous books, including *The End of The Nation State: The Rise of Regional Economies.*

### Cem Özdemir
Bündnis 90/Die Grünen, Berlin

Born in 1965 into a family of Turkish immigrants. After training as a teacher, studied social education in Reutlingen. Since 1981 member of Bündnis 90/Die Grünen, 1989-1995 member of the Baden-Württemberg party leadership. Elected to the German Bundestag in 1994. From 1998 to 2002, parliamentary party spokesman on internal affairs. Chairman of the German-Turkish parliamentary group, awarded the Civis Prize and the Theodor Heuss Medal in 1996. Author of a number of books.

### Quentin Peel
International Affairs Editor, Financial Times, London

Born in 1948. Studied French, German and economics at Cambridge University before starting his career in journalism. Joined the *Financial Times* in 1975 and became South Africa correspondent in Johannesburg in 1976. Africa editor 1981-1984, and then European Community correspondent in Brussels 1984-1987. Moscow correspondent 1988-1991 during perestroika, and bureau chief in Germany 1991-1994. In 1994 returned to London as foreign editor before taking up his present position in 1998. Writes a regular column on European affairs and transatlantic relations.

## THE SPEAKERS

### Wolfgang Schäuble
MP, CDU, Former Federal Minister, Berlin

Born in 1942 in Freiburg. Studied law and economics in Freiburg and Hamburg, doctorate in 1971. Member of the Christian Democratic Union (CDU) since 1965. Since 1972 member of the German parliament. 1981-1984 Parliamentary Secretary of the CDU/CSU parliamentary group. Then Federal Minister for Special Tasks and head of the federal Chancellery until 1989, after that Federal Minister of the Interior until 1991. 1991-2000 chairman of the CDU/CSU parliamentary group in the German parliament. 1998-2000 chairman of the CDU. Member of the executive committee of the CDU since April 2000.

© Dieter Bauer

### Peter Scholl-Latour
Author and Journalist, Paris

Born 1924 in Bochum, Germany. Degree in Political Science from the Institut National des Sciences Politiques in Paris and in Arabic and Islamic Studies from the Lebanese University of Beirut. Doctorate from the Sorbonne, Paris. Active as a journalist since 1950. Among his many postings: correspondent in Africa and Indochina, head of the German TV studio in Paris, executive director of the WDR TV channel and publisher of the German weekly magazine *Stern*. Author of many best-selling publications, including *Der Tod im Reisfeld*; *Das Schwert des Islam*; *Eine Welt in Auflösung*; *Lügen im Heiligen Land* and *Afrikanische Totenklage*.

### Martin Schulze
Journalist, Berlin

Born in 1937 in Essen. Studied physics and philosophy in Tübingen, Bonn and Berlin. After his studies, worked as a journalist for several German dailies, and as a film author and editor for "Report" and "Weltspiegel". 1989-1993 ARD editor-in-chief, 1993-1995 ARD special correspondent in the Bonn studio. Became head of the ARD TV studio in Bonn and chief correspondent for the ARD. Since 2000, presenter for Phoenix, since 2002 presenter of the "Berliner/Bonner Phoenix-Runde".

### Barry Steinhardt
Associate Director, American Civil Liberties Union, New York

Born in 1953. Graduated in 1978 from Northeastern University School of Law. Since 1992 has served as Associate Director of the American Civil Liberties Union. Recently named to head ACLU's new programme on Civil Liberties and Technology. Co-founder of the Global Internet Liberty Campaign, the international coalition of NGOs concerned with the rights of Internet users. Member of the Blue Ribbon Panel on Genetics of the National Conference of State Legislatures. Has spoken and published widely on privacy, free expression and information technology issues.

# THE SPEAKERS

### Natan Sznaider
Professor of Sociology, The Academic College of Tel Aviv-Yaffo

Born in 1954 in Mannheim. Emigrated 1974 to Israel where he studied and continues to live and work. Professor of Sociology and Cultural Studies at the Academic College in Tel Aviv. Writes regularly for the *Süddeutsche Zeitung* and is the author of several books. He recently published *The Compassionate Temperament* and, in German, *Erinnerung im Globalen Zeitalter*.

### Museji Ahmed Takolia
Senior Adviser, Diversity Strategy & Equal Opportunities,
Cabinet Office, Government of the United Kingdom, London

Born in 1960 in Coventry, England. B.A. in education (Hons), University of Cambridge; M.A. in social sciences, University of Bristol; and Executive Education Programme Fellow, Princeton University. Highly respected authority on diversity and equality policy. Has advised local and central governments in the UK, South Africa and USA. Commissioner on the Commission for Health Improvement. Member of the Governing Executive of Ruskin College, Oxford.

### Ilija Trojanow
Writer, Sofia/Mumbai

Born in 1965 in Sofia. In 1972 the family managed to flee to Italy. Applied for political asylum in Germany, later granted citizenship and lived in Munich. Lived ten years in Kenya, and worked as a publisher of African literature. Made his name as a writer with his book *Die Welt ist groß und Rettung lauert überall*. Lives and works as a free-lance journalist and author in Mumbai.

### Gianni Vattimo
MEP, Party of European Socialists, Strasbourg/Brussels

Born in 1936. Professor for Theoretical Philosophy at the University of Turin and Member of the European Parliament in Brussels. He is publisher of the scientific magazines *Revista di Estetica* and *Filosofia*. Member of the scientific advisory council to numerous technical journals and of the "Accademia delle Scienze". Regularly comments on general philosophical questions and current political issues in the Italian daily *La Stampa*. In 2002, recipient of the Hannah Arendt Prize.

# The Alfred Herrhausen Society for International Dialogue

## Members of the Board of Trustees

Dr. Josef Ackermann (Chairman), Frankfurt/Main
Prof. Jean-Christophe Ammann, Frankfurt/Main
Prof. Sybille Ebert-Schifferer, Rome
Prof. Wolfgang Frühwald, Bonn
Dr. Tessen von Heydebreck, Frankfurt/Main
H.E. Ambassador Wolfgang Ischinger, Washington
Jürgen Jeske, Frankfurt/Main
Dr. Josef Joffe, Hamburg
Hans Werner Kilz, Munich
Prof. Joachim-Felix Leonhard, Munich
GMD Ingo Metzmacher, Hamburg
Prof. Eckard Minx, Berlin
Rabbi Julia Neuberger, London
Min. Dir. Wolfgang Nowak, Berlin
Prof. Christoph Schwöbel, Heidelberg

## Managing Directors

Dr. Walter Homolka (Chairman), Frankfurt/Main
Hanns Michael Hölz, Frankfurt/Main
Prof. Norbert Walter, Frankfurt/Main

## Executive Director

Maike Tippmann M.A., Frankfurt/Main